CLARKE MURPHY

Russell Reynolds Associates

sustainable
leadership

LESSONS OF VISION, COURAGE, AND GRIT FROM THE CEOS

WHO DARED TO BUILD A BETTER WORLD

WILEY

Published by John Wiley & Sons, Inc., Hoboken, New Jersey.
Published simultaneously in Canada.

Limit of Liability/Disclaimer of Warranty: While the publisher and author have used their best efforts in preparing this book, they make no representations or warranties with respect to the accuracy or completeness of the contents of this book and specifically disclaim any implied warranties of merchantability or fitness for a particular purpose. No warranty may be created or extended by sales representatives or written sales materials. The advice and strategies contained herein may not be suitable for your situation. You should consult with a professional where appropriate. Further, readers should be aware that websites listed in this work may have changed or disappeared between when this work was written and when it is read. Neither the publisher nor authors shall be liable for any loss of profit or any other commercial damages, including but not limited to special, incidental, consequential, or other damages.

For general information on our other products and services or for technical support, please contact our Customer Care Department within the United States at (800) 762-2974, outside the United States at (317) 572-3993 or fax (317) 572-4002.

Wiley also publishes its books in a variety of electronic formats. Some content that appears in print may not be available in electronic formats. For more information about Wiley products, visit our web site at www.wiley.com.

Library of Congress Cataloging-in-Publication Data

Names: Murphy, Clarke, author.
Title: Sustainable leadership : lessons of vision, courage, and grit from
 the CEOs who dared to build a better world / Clarke Murphy, Russell
 Reynolds Associates.
Description: Hoboken, New Jersey : John Wiley & Sons, Inc., [2022] |
 Includes bibliographical references and index.
Identifiers: LCCN 2022029445 (print) | LCCN 2022029446 (ebook) | ISBN
 9781119872153 (hardback) | ISBN 9781119872177 (adobe pdf) | ISBN
 9781119872160 (epub)
Subjects: LCSH: Chief executive officers. | Social responsibility of
 business. | Corporate culture. | Sustainable development. | Career
 development.
Classification: LCC HD38.2 .M873 2022 (print) | LCC HD38.2 (ebook) | DDC
 658.4/2—dc23/eng/20220624
LC record available at https://lccn.loc.gov/2022029445
LC ebook record available at https://lccn.loc.gov/2022029446

Cover design: Russell Reynolds Associates
Cover image: © Katsumi Murouchi/Getty Images

SKY10034758_072822

To the unnamed and unsung sustainable leaders not mentioned on these pages—the individuals who have yet to be promoted or developed as future CEOs and board members. If we accelerate their careers, if they can follow some of the examples and takeaways written here, collectively they will improve the way the world is led.

Contents

Foreword

By ADENA T. Friedman, President & CEO of Nasdaq, Inc.

Almost no topic inspires more passion and urgency from stakeholders as the drive for sustainability. Individually and collectively we all have a part to play in protecting the health and long-term sustainability of our shared planet, and in creating thriving economies and communities in which everyone can participate and succeed.

Within this context, business plays an important and defining role. In recent years, we have seen the growth of capital market participation at a scale and level of diversity like never before. This increased participation has also brought new expectations for companies and the role they can play in addressing societal challenges. Employees, investors, and consumers want to grow their wealth and savings, but they also care about *how* corporations make those returns and their broader impact. This underscores that sustainability and profitability are not competing forces—they are an "and," not an "or."

Many people know Nasdaq as the largest global equities marketplace for innovative companies. But, Nasdaq today is also the premier platform and ecosystem for the global financial system. In addition to our foundational marketplaces business, we provide the technology that powers more than 130 markets around the world. This gives me a privileged position of being able to view the breadth of global business and engage with leaders across the financial ecosystem, from corporates to asset owners, asset managers, other market operators, and beyond. Without question, sustainability continues to be a top agenda item across the board, and there are clear and encouraging signs that business is responding to the challenge.

Nasdaq helps get capital into the hands of the most cutting-edge companies, many of which are focused on creating sustainable solutions for the future. We enable any investor to support a sustainable economy by betting on these bold pioneers—and they are doing just that in unprecedented numbers. We are also seeing more companies than ever embrace environmental, social, and governance principles and make net-zero commitments.

As sustainability becomes a significant focus for business, we are defining the best practices that will drive future success. It requires a willingness to set meaningful goals and be held accountable for them. It requires the ability to prioritize long-term social and environmental benefits that may not be realized for decades to come. It requires flexibility and understanding as the space evolves and matures. Perhaps most importantly, it requires leaders who can recognize the role business can play in creating a more equitable and sustainable world.

Clarke Murphy's insights are based upon face-to-face conversations with individuals who are in the leadership seats influencing and shaping this change. He is right there in the trenches with the actual decision makers. By asking the questions others don't think to ask, he has discovered exactly the kind of mindset, skillset, vision, and drive it takes to lead a corporation into a sustainable future. Through rich storytelling and exclusive insights from the world's most influential CEOs and the next generation of leaders and startup pioneers, he details the steps we can all take to move toward our sustainability goals. The advice and examples found on the next pages demonstrate that it's not in the talking, but the doing.

Through his experience and expertise, Clarke is able to draw out personal and life-changing experiences from CEOs, crystallizing their deepest thoughts into actionable takeaways. I should know—I've had those conversations with Clarke myself, and he has been a guiding and encouraging voice.

So, it comes as no surprise to me that Clarke gets others to open up in his book, which often feels like having an intimate conversation around the conference room table with some of the most brilliant minds in business. Like many of the insightful leaders he speaks with, Clarke has the humility and learning quotient to listen and learn. Each chapter is an education on how these leaders exceeded their goalposts on myriad sustainability issues, from developing clean fuel for container ships to helping women farmers of India improve their lives by cultivating guar beans for consumer products. There is a sense of urgency as we learn what's being done now, and how leaders are developing talent to accelerate change in the near and distant future. Above all, we come away with a profound understanding of what's possible and the inspiration to charge boldly forward.

Acknowledgments

WITH SO MANY inspiring individuals along the way who encouraged, supported, and helped shape my thinking for this book, it is difficult to know where to start. It all began before that fateful snowy day in Davos, when my partners, Simon Kingston and Hans Reus, urged me to meet with Lise Kingo—a career gamechanger for me. There would be no book without that meeting of minds.

And the team at RRA, including Amy Scissons, who has championed this book idea from the beginning, and Tom Handcock for his outstanding work with the United Nations Global Compact to develop our Sustainable Leadership blueprint. Tom, your talents for turning data and concepts into fascinating content is remarkable. Maja Hadziomerovic and Vanessa Di Matteo, your thorough research was on point, enabling some amazing exchanges with some of the world's most insightful corporate leaders. And our resident wordsmith, Susie Sell, whose patience, humor, and organization is astounding. She gave birth to this book and her daughter simultaneously! To Samantha Marshall, the collaborator/magician who crafted flowing prose from disjointed interview notes.

Not least, I would like to thank all those CEOs, CSOs, and board members, named and unnamed on these pages, who took the time to invest in the legacies of others, generously sharing their own experiences to accelerate the development of the next generation of sustainable leaders.

Finally, to the Murphy family, whose love and support has been the greatest gift in this project, matched only by a tremendous collective sense of humor. *Fortis et hospitalis!*

Introduction:
A Meeting of Minds

We cannot solve our problems with the same thinking we used when we created them.

—*Albert Einstein*

I WAS BEGINNING to wonder, What the heck am I doing here?

For years I had resisted the idea of going to Davos, the annual week-long retreat for the powerful, wealthy, and famous—heads of state, business leaders, Nobel prize–winning economists and celebrities from around the globe. My company, Russell Reynolds Associates (RRA), works with many of these business executives in the form of leadership consulting and searches for their C-suite executives. But the World Economic Forum's A-list attendees go there to hobnob with each other, not meet one of their service providers. I have always believed one should be the speaker, not the sponsor, at major conferences. It was only after several of my European partners insisted, informing me that the event was beginning to open up to different kinds of thought leaders such as nongovernmental organizations (NGOs) and activists on pressing issues such as climate change, diversity, and poverty, that I finally agreed to go.

I arrived in the middle of one of the worst snowstorms that this isolated ski resort town in the heart of the Swiss Alps had seen in almost three decades. The main theme of Davos that year was global

1

responsibility. But, in January 2019, my second time at Davos, the topic on everyone's minds was the weather. I'd taken the bus from Zurich, which was a mistake. It took five hours, including a stop to put snow chains on the tires, and there was no bathroom onboard. But I was one of the lucky ones. Blizzard-like conditions eventually closed the airport, leaving hundreds of attendees stranded. Those of us who managed to find our way there were left to trudge through the thick blanket of snow that covered Dammstrasse, the main street of Davos. Even Al Gore had to cancel his helicopter, then motorcade up the mountain. Taxis were scarce; everyone was running late. Fortunately, I remembered to pack a decent pair of boots, which allowed me to dash between appointments of 15-minute increments—the time allotted to get deals done or make my desired impact on the CEO with whom I was scheduled to meet.

Much to my relief, I had many amazing conversations that week. One unique aspect of Davos is that its attendees don't walk around with an army of handlers because it's understood that security is high around the perimeter. It makes people like French president Emmanuel Macron or UN Secretary General António Guterres or then–managing director of the International Monetary Fund Christine Lagarde entirely approachable if you feel brave enough. The worst that can happen is a polite brush-off. At least you won't get shoved out of the way by a bodyguard.

But, for all that accessibility, rich Swiss food, and bracing mountain air, nothing about Davos thus far had necessarily blown me away. I was focused on cementing some of our existing strong relationships and laying foundations for new ones. Klaus Schwab, founder and president of the World Economic Forum, told us on the opening night, "We have a unique chance here in Davos to show the world that we are devoting our energies and our resources to creating a global economy that serves the interests of humankind." That message resonated with me, and I hoped it was true.

By the end of my fourth day, I lost track of how many people with whom I had already met. It was a dizzying number of appointments, and one of the last on my schedule was with Lise Kingo, a Danish businesswoman who was then CEO and president of the United Nations Global Compact (UNGC).

Back in 2000, the UN formed a nonbinding pact to encourage corporations around the globe to adopt a set of 17 Sustainable Development Goals (SDGs)—from wastewater reduction to more equitable workplace policies—to be met by 2030. More than 10,000 companies, including RRA, had put their names to the mission but getting them to put pledge into practice had proven to be a mammoth undertaking, and the 2020 deadline for a progress report was looming.

I only knew Lise by reputation. Our firm had recruited her, but we'd never met.

My partners, Simon Kingston and Hans Reus, were adamant that Lise and I meet, in hopes of developing a closer relationship. She was a scholar who'd penned multiple papers on the topics of sustainability and business, as well as an experienced international business executive. Highly respected among world leaders across industries and nationalities, and especially skilled at bringing along even the most reluctant stakeholders, she was best known for her pioneering of the "triple bottom line"—balancing economic, social, and environmental priorities. Lise has, for example, played an integral role in developing the "Changing Diabetes" corporate brand, including the Diabetes Barometer index during her long executive tenure at Scandinavian pharmaceutical giant Novo Nordisk, raising awareness about the disease and improving patient care, while also driving for profits. Her business savvy combined with a dedication to social responsibility and sustainability had even been recognized by the Dow Jones Sustainability Index, making her the perfect person to helm the UN Global Compact.

Lise's Davos office, located inside "The Sustainable Impact Hub"—a makeshift workspace about 600 meters away from the main Congress building—was a hive of activity where NGO and UN representatives buzzed around from meeting to meeting with world leaders and each other. The UNGC didn't have the funds for a marquee location, and with just two meeting spaces allocated to more than 10 of these nonprofits and their dozens of delegates, I walked into the middle of a maelstrom.

At first, I couldn't even find Lise as I wandered through a maze of frosted glass and NGO signage. I asked around and was eventually told that she was still deep in a conversation with the president of Ghana. (Lise was obviously a woman in high demand.) Prior to that she'd been face-to-face with various CEOs of companies that were members of the UNGC, from Unilever to Nike to Coca-Cola. (I could not have felt less relevant.) Her meetings, like everyone else's that week, had run overtime. So I waited. And waited. That 15-minute increment became 30 minutes, then 45 minutes. Finally, I sent her a text.

"If this is a bad time, we can always reschedule," I said, admittedly feeling a little frustrated.

"No, no, no, please!" she said. "Wait right there. I'm coming out now!"

And within seconds Lise appeared from behind a partition, right where I happened to be standing. Lise was simultaneously mortified, charming, and profusely apologetic. She immediately ushered me into her office, which was the size of a broom closet, or what she jokingly referred to as her "monk's cell." As we squeezed around the table she apologized again, this time for not being able to offer me a coffee. Lise was disarmingly sincere—one of those individuals with whom I felt an immediate connection.

"I've been looking forward to our talk all day!" she exclaimed, wasting no time to get to the point.

"Clarke, I am distraught," she confessed.

"Why?" I asked.

"Because in 2020 I will have to stand in front of the United Nations, the world, and explain why we are nowhere near reaching our sustainability goals. For all our grand ambitions, our corporate partners have so little to show for it. What am I going to say?!"

For the next few minutes, Lise vented her frustration over the lack of progress while I listened, feeling like an undergraduate getting a crash course from a professor on the critical role that public-private partnerships must play in the well-being of people and planet. It was evident that there was a huge gap between what leaders of the great companies of the world were saying and what they were accomplishing. The intention and commitment were there, but the momentum that UNGC was building was falling way short of the changes the world needed.

Lise went into more detail about how the UNGC was attempting to help corporations reach the SDGs. One of its largest ambitions, set forth in the Paris Climate Agreement in 2015, is to cap global warming at 1.5 degrees Celsius by 2030. To these ends, the UNGC asks companies to first do business responsibly and then pursue opportunities to solve societal challenges through business innovation and collaboration. In that moment Lise and I first met, it was evident that a kind of inertia was holding back this potential progress.

"You know, Clarke, we are facing this massive increase in the earth's temperature if nothing changes, yet there is no sense of urgency. Why?"

Lise and I talked for a while, trying to figure out what was missing. There was awareness of sustainability, sure, but it wasn't translating into action. Sustainability wasn't being integrated throughout organizations, and major decisions and actions weren't being taken through the lens of goals such as human rights or diversity or improving the quality of the air we breathe. Instead of being part of a core strategy, sustainability was being relegated to a single initiative, department, or function. Instead of being seen as an opportunity to further the growth of the business, it was being viewed as a function of risk management or virtual signaling for consumers and other stakeholders. Sustainability wasn't being seen as a source for value creation as much as a box to be ticked.

And that's when it hit us. The transition toward sustainable business is so much more than the right pledges, plans, programs, or words on a page. It's about leadership. It's a distinctly human endeavor.

You could have all the right language and commitment statements, with sustainability programs lined up, and still fail. If you don't have an inspired and inspiring leader at the top, it's not going to happen.

We were onto something. No one seemed to be talking about the role of leaders in making the shift toward stakeholder capitalism. We needed to build a generation of sustainable leaders with the right mindset and skills to help solve the world's challenges while balancing other stakeholders' needs for long-term financial returns. We needed these leaders to be engaged at the strategic level. And we needed a sense of urgency and ambition, because actions taken by corporations ripple outward, affecting people, planet, and prosperity across borders and far beyond what any individual, or even government, could do.

So how could we help? How could we encourage, cajole, and inspire corporate leaders to step up to the plate? Perhaps UNGC and RRA could together ring the bell on leadership.

We needed to be able to demonstrate what sustainable leadership looks like with real-world, present-day examples of sustainability luminaries. The good news is that those leaders exist. The more we talked, the more we realized that we were rich in examples of corporate executives—cosigners of the UNGC—who've made extraordinary strides toward sustainability goals and unambiguously demonstrated that it's possible to do good in the world while not just continuing to keep the lights on but outstripping their competition by significant margins.

The trick was to decode their DNA, breaking down what was working, understanding not just what their goals were, but how they embedded them into their daily operations and got buy-in from their stakeholders, not least their employees all the way down to the plant floor or shopfront, who would act on the companies' sustainable policies long after their CEOs retired or moved on. How do you embed that passion into an organization's culture so that it guides the decision-making on everything from where to invest, to what to cut, and whom to hire? How do you accelerate the numbers and success of leaders who care about sustainability so that the pyramid grows exponentially and the actions take over? What are the core values and mindset of the leaders at the very top, and how can their actions create a legacy of sustainability action?

This was where I came in. At RRA, understanding what makes great leaders perform is what we do. Our mission has always been to find CEOs, C-suite executives, and board directors whose ethos goes beyond short-term financial goals and who understand the importance not just of a happy and healthy workforce but also the wider worlds in which they operate. We have the metrics and experience to drill down into the character and skillsets of some of the most powerful and impactful leaders on the planet. Collectively, our team has spent hundreds of thousands of hours asking the thought-provoking questions that can lead to the most profound, *aha* moments in the conversation.

By the end of my meeting with Lise, I was fired up. I finally understood what our role in this burning issue of sustainability could be. Applying our knowledge of the anatomy of great leadership, we would do the research, partnering with UNGC to highlight those pioneers who are moving the dial forward and not only meeting, but exceeding goals on climate change, diversity, poverty alleviation, access to health care, technology, and a whole host of other global issues that cannot be solved by individuals alone.

Global businesses have the resources and human power to right this ship in tangible, practical ways that will be seen and felt for generations to come. They can concretely demonstrate the benefit of sustainability to all their stakeholders so that everyone can get behind their goals. Although these corporate leaders aren't the only important actors as we face down these existential challenges, it's my humble opinion that they play the starring role.

As our 15 minutes turned into 45 minutes, Lise and I agreed to continue our conversation beyond the rarefied air of that Alpine resort town. It turned out that we lived and worked a mere few blocks from each other in New York City. We even shared a favorite restaurant—Orsay—where we agreed to meet next. This was just the beginning of what would become a beautiful collaboration and friendship.

The first fruits of this partnership were a comprehensive study of CEOs and board members across continents and industries with a notable track record of making progress toward sustainability goals in tandem with commercial results. We selected these leaders based on detailed metrics, such as being actively engaged in the UN Global Compact and measuring their companies' performance against a "control group" of other Fortune 500 CEOs with poor sustainability rankings. Our interview subjects have made progress where others have not, with tangible evidence that their sustainable leadership methods are moving the needle forward in ways that are much louder than mere words.

We then conducted in-depth interviews with these individuals, along with background analysis, probing into their motivations, experience, and capabilities, as well as actions they have taken to embed sustainability into their overall business strategies, culture, and leadership talent pipelines—all combined with strong business performance. Based on this information goldmine, and with the input of chief sustainability officers from seven of the largest corporations in the world, we developed a first-of-its-kind diagnostic framework of sustainable leadership, along with analysis that defines the characteristics, actions, and differentiating leadership attributes that fuel a sustainable leader's success.

The most successful leaders all had a sustainability mindset, combined with four specific competencies. We defined the sustainable mindset as a purpose-driven belief that business is not just a commercial activity divorced from the wider societal and environmental context in which it operates. To be successful these leaders must manage and innovate for commercial, environmental, and social outcomes (people, planet, and profit) by integrating these core values and beliefs into their strategy and operations.

Alongside their sustainable mindset, these leaders also possessed four specific capabilities. You will read about these core features in the coming chapters but here they are in a nutshell:

Multilevel systems thinking, which integrates economic, societal, and environmental factors into a purpose-driven strategy, turning sustainability into competitive advantage

Stakeholder inclusion, where leaders do not seek to manage stakeholders but actively include them in defining and executing decisions; even competitors should be considered partners and stakeholders when it comes to sustainability

Disruptive innovation, by courageously challenging traditional approaches while cutting through bureaucracy and doing away with the profitability/sustainability trade-off

Long-term activation, setting audacious business and sustainability goals, and driving concerted action while staying the course in the face of setbacks or pushback

The end result of our collaboration was a landmark report, titled, "Leadership for a Decade of Action" and released at the UNGC's 20th Anniversary Leaders' Summit on June 15, 2020, which made the business case for sustainability, showing rather than telling how it could be done, with a healthy blend of pragmatism, realism, and optimism. And Lise no longer had to stand in front of these delegates with nothing to say!

"Transforming our world is all about leadership," Lise said in her remarks at the summit. "As we set out to recover better from COVID-19, the fragile nature of our progress to meet the 2030 deadline to transform our world means that incorporating sustainability across strategy and operations is not only the right thing to do, it's the smart thing to do. We need leaders everywhere to step up their ambition and become agents for sustainable change. This is the moment for top management and boards to ensure that these critical competencies are represented and developed across the organization."

Just as we'd completed our deep dive into the subject of sustainable leadership, the world began to wake up, aided by a series of natural disasters turned cataclysmic by climate change. The Amazon rainforest wildfires, where more than 80,000 fires across Brazil had been stoked by slash-and-burn farming, could be seen from outer space. If that wasn't enough to jolt humankind into action, there were the California wildfires, Typhoon Hagibis in Japan, flooding in the American Midwest on a biblical scale, Cyclone Idai in southern Africa, and, from September 2019 to March 2020, Australia's bushfire season, which was the worst on record, resulting in unforgettable images of burnt and maimed koala bears, kangaroos, and other wildlife. Suddenly, sustainability was the trending topic, high on the list at the next Davos and the one after that, where Lise's once-modest UN and NGO hive had moved to center stage, with thought leaders on the topic now enjoying well-deserved prominence at the World Economic Forum's marquee locations and events.

It's been enormously heartening to witness this shift in attitude, not to mention financial commitment. Business and global leaders finally understand that sustainability is a leadership imperative—a must-have versus window dressing that does nothing to fundamentally alter the course of the business. They understand that sustainability is mission critical and that the time to act is now.

This book will provide the practical takeaways to implement whatever sustainability goals make the most sense for you and your organization, whether you are leading a nonprofit or championing ESG goals at your firm. Through storytelling and insights from some of the most impactful CEOs of the most significant multinational organizations, including Heineken, Adidas, Maersk, and Accenture, among others, as well as real-world examples from the trenches, you will see what the results of sustainable leadership look like in the real world. You will discover how Aurélia Nguyen, managing director of

COVAX, led a modern-day equivalent of the Berlin airlift by giving millions in underdeveloped countries access to the COVID vaccine. Or how Ms. Farzanah Chowdhury, managing director and CEO of Green Delta Insurance Company Limited in Bangladesh, leveraged technology to give women access to financial literacy and independence.

At RRA, we are fortunate enough to have front-row seats and unrivalled insights into these leaders' strategies, values, passions, and personalities. You will learn directly from the mouths of these accomplished global leaders exactly what goes into their decision-making process and how they scale their sustainable leadership mindset, making it central to their organization's culture.

I will share the specifics of what that looks like in terms of people, product, processes, partnerships, and profits. In other words, these next pages will not only take you inside the mind of a sustainable leader but also provide you with their lessons learned on how to build that next generation so that, as you transition toward new economic models, sustainability becomes your legacy—a guiding force of the business and its workforce well into the future. Equally, their stories will be an opportunity to learn from their mistakes made on this journey.

The sustainable leadership movement is growing, and you must be a part of it. The mission of our firm is to improve the way the world is led, and sustainability is at the forefront of that goal. The purpose of this book is to exponentially multiply the 55 pioneers we identified in our original research into tens of thousands of next-generation sustainable leaders through engaging, detailed, and candid storytelling about mistakes made and lessons learned.

We can strike gold by focusing more on the next generation, who are ready, willing, and able to move into action on sustainability goals. Our research revealed that this group is fast becoming the engine room of real transformation, and there are people in organizations today who have already taken on multiple initiatives to improve environmental outcomes, for example. Based on the passion and real-world experience delivering sustainability results of those young leaders who will ascend to the C-suite, the future looks bright.

On these next pages, you'll learn exactly how your organization, whatever its size, can become a part of this revolution. You could be the CEO of a Fortune 500 company, the founder of a startup, the owner of a family business, an employee on a management track, or a student of business, in any part of the world, and have a broad and meaningful impact. You need not be a born believer, and, in fact, few CEOs are. Many come to this along the way, becoming not just passionate advocates, but actors with impact. Nor does it matter what industry you are in or where exactly you are in your career trajectory, your decisions and actions today will determine your legacy as a sustainable leader well into the future.

The sustainable leadership principles and processes you will discover are universal, cutting across geographies, cultures, and sectors. They can be learned, developed, and cascaded throughout multiple business functions. You will know exactly what it takes to drive sustainability into the core of an organization. You will gain insight into what it is that sets those leaders apart who have succeeded, what are the actions they have taken and the lessons they have learned.

And, by the end of the last chapter, you will walk away feeling just as I did as I left for my next appointment after that fateful meeting of minds on a snowy mid-winter's day in Davos—energized and filled with hope.

PART

I

Why the World Needs Sustainable Leaders

1

A Sense of Urgency

We have left it too late to solve this dilemma with a graduated response.
Emergency action, akin to putting the economy on a war footing, remains
essential.
                    —*Ian Dunlop, former senior executive, Royal Dutch Shell, 2016*

A RIVER FULL of coal ash. That's what Lynn Good, CEO of Duke
Energy, had to face six months into her job as leader of the largest
utility in the United States. On February 2, 2014, security guards at
the Duke Energy Dan River Steam Station in Eden, North Carolina,
noticed liquified coal ash leaking from a buried stormwater pipe. Coal
ash is the gray, powdery by-product of burning coal that's used to
produce energy. The drainage pipe had spewed nearly 40,000 tons of
the slurry into the Dan River, along with 27 million gallons of
wastewater that had been released from an old coal plant that had,
ironically, been shut down two years earlier.

This was, potentially, an ecological and human disaster. It took a
week to seal the broken pipe, by which time the ash had made its way
almost 70 miles from the original site. The river, which was a source of

drinking water for the communities along its banks, as well as a haven for anglers and nature lovers, now had traces of arsenic, lead, zinc, iron, selenium, and other poisonous metals and chemicals. Fortunately, the immediate fears that fish and wildlife, including endangered species, might be killed were never realized. But Duke Energy would have to manage the damage to the company's reputation for years afterwards.

Lynn and I have been friends for a number of years. We first met when we advised the board of Duke Energy on its CEO succession. Lynn was CFO at the time and was eventually selected as chief executive. (Duke Energy had the distinction of having both a female CEO and a female chair, Ann Gray.) An accountant by training, Lynn was among the few female partners at two big accounting firms, Arthur Andersen & Co. and Deloitte. A self-described "numbers gal," she is dispassionately analytical, yet at the same time deeply empathetic toward the people she manages.

"How did you feel when you were faced with that scene?" I asked Lynn about the ash spill, seven years later. "It must have been one heck of a rough start to your new job!"

"It had a profound impact on me," Lynn explained. Against the advice of many, she immediately drove to the site to inspect the damage for herself. "The enormity of what had happened actually hit home before I could even step out of the car."

The gentleman in charge of Duke Energy's fossil hydro division came up to her car window looking stricken. Lynn could have sworn she saw tears in his eyes. She quickly rolled down her window and looked up at him as he spoke in a voice hoarse with emotion and fumes: "We will fix this; I promise," he told her.

Lynn was acutely aware of the emotional devastation this environmental disaster had caused her team—a workforce that strove for operational excellence and total reliability. That moment crystallized how deeply the team at Duke Energy wanted the company to be both sustainable *and* reliable. Duke Energy was made up of multiple generations of family members and enjoyed a culture of enormous pride. This era of sustainability would be an extension of that corporate pride.

All at once the company was in the crosshairs of environmental activists, federal agencies, and the media. But this tragic incident would reinforce its journey toward becoming an industry leader in clean, green energy. The executive team on down, Duke Energy intensified its long-standing focus on sustainability, with Lynn's unflagging support and guidance.

■ ■ ■

Duke Energy, under Lynn Good's leadership, heard the clarion call of sustainable business and began the challenging work of washing the "dirty face of coal" several years earlier than most. She began the often-painful task of closing fossil-fueled plants, phasing out coal, and transitioning to more renewable forms of energy while giving teams in those business units the opportunity to retrain, relocate, and grow along with the organization.

Duke Energy also funded an innovation center that, among many other things, tests out green energy solutions for its customers. They also started a program (in partnership with Accenture and Microsoft) to buy satellite imagery and use drones to spot methane leaks with much greater efficiency than hand-held detectors. Lynn paid close attention to her team leaders across all areas of the business, seeking real engagement on what was needed to achieve the dual missions of the company—reliability and sustainability—while also reinforcing the importance of customer affordability. I will delve into more detail about Lynn's transformation strategy later in this book. Suffice to say it was a multipronged effort that took equal parts persistence, patience, and unwavering commitment.

"In my mind, it's building a workforce that can make change, which in this case happens to be around climate and sustainability," Lynn shared with me. "I want people who are willing to challenge [the] status quo, someone who is more interested in how it can be done versus how it used to be done. Someone who spends time looking outside for solutions, as opposed to just inside. Someone who can catalyze a team of people to go after a big complex assignment, where you don't know what the exact result will be, but you make progress along the way. You stop early when it looks like a failure, and you have the resilience to pivot and keep going on something new."

It's advice that leaders from a broad cross-section of industries could use. Even those who may not have even seen themselves as bad actors on the global stage are recognizing that they have a role to play in addressing the world's challenges and that the time to act is long overdue. Sustainability has emerged as the defining issue of our time. It is no longer a nice-to-have; it's a *must*-have.

Achieving the level of transformation necessary to avert profound global crises takes leaders like Lynn who have vision and grit. With corporations under growing pressure to look beyond quarterly performance and profits to deliver true long-term value for all stakeholders—employees, customers, suppliers, and members of the general public affected by their decisions—simply appointing a chief sustainability officer, although an important step, is not enough. There needs to be a wholesale embrace of sustainability at all levels of an organization and across every function.

And yet, according to our *Divides and Dividends* report[1] at RRA, which delves into action steps that can be taken for a sustainable future, only 43% of C-suite leaders globally say their organization has a sustainability strategy in place that has been acted on and clearly communicated, and only 51% believe their CEO is personally committed to advancing sustainability goals or can point to progress. (Employees are even more skeptical, with just 26% recognizing CEO commitment.) When asked about the driving force behind their company's approach to sustainability, 45% of C-suite leaders cited brand management—they want to be viewed as socially responsible or use sustainability for competitive differentiation. And a mere 21% say that value creation sets the agenda.

While CEOs flounder, the world's challenges continue to escalate. We're on track for a 3.5-degree Celsius rise in temperature this century based on current commitments (UNEP 2019 Emissions Gap Report[2]) and 14 million tons of plastics continue to enter our oceans every year, according to the International Union for Conservation of Nature.[3]

The 2019–2022 global pandemic laid bare even more of the vulnerabilities humanity faces, from access to health care and vaccines to supply chain chaos and financial hardship from lockdowns and unemployment. As a result, the legitimacy of major commercial enterprises, and the people who lead them, is coming into question like never before. A vast swathe of stakeholders—including customers, employees, investors, and suppliers—are challenging companies to respond to changing societal values, concerns about climate change, the depletion of finite natural resources, and the political instability that goes along with these social and economic inequities.

Bernard Looney, CEO of multinational oil and gas company bp, and one of the many leaders you will hear from later in this book, has taken note of the shift in consciousness around the world: "That's what society is expecting, and I'm not here to fight society. You cannot go against the grain of society and expect to be a long-term successful company."[4]

The Trust Deficit

Consider the results of the January 2020 global marketing survey—the "Edelman Trust Barometer"—where more than half of respondents reported that capitalism in its current form is doing more harm than good.[5] A few months later, respondents pointed to a growing sense of inequity, with 67% of those sampled agreeing that those with less money and education have unfairly suffered most from the risk of illness and the need to sacrifice due to the pandemic. Less than a third thought global CEOs were doing a good job of responding to the shifting needs of consumers and other stakeholders during the pandemic.[6]

And yet, by the time Edelman had conducted its 2021 trust survey, when we were further along the trajectory of the pandemic, public perception of CEOs had shifted. Trust in news sources and government agencies had plummeted to all-time lows due to an epidemic of misinformation, leaving businesses as the only institutions that are trusted as competent and ethical, according to 61% of respondents. A stunning 86% of respondents said CEOs must lead on societal issues, and 68% want businesses to take charge when government fails to fix these problems.[7]

Spreading the Word

One example of businesses stepping into the breach to communicate about sustainability is occurring in the beauty and wellness industries. In 2021, Brazil-based beauty group Natura &Co, which owns Natura, Avon, The Body Shop, and Aesop, became a founding member of the WaterBear Network, a free streaming platform that promotes environmental awareness and action. Natura &Co will showcase content such as documentaries on the Amazon through its own dedicated channel, promoting advocacy through storytelling. The beauty brand plans to educate the public at large through "inspiring content" about climate change, human rights, and embracing full circularity of its use of resources by 2030.

My own takeaway from these survey numbers is that business leaders now have a strong mandate to step up, fill the void, and lead on broader societal issues that go far beyond their corporate footprints. These CEOs, board directors, executives, and team managers are facing heightened expectations to use their intellect and energy to deliver solutions to the many existential problems we face as a global community.

To answer that call, a new level of ambition is needed, combined with a sense of urgency.

"We have a rare and short window of opportunity to rebuild our world for the better, and therefore we need to focus more than ever to ensure that our post-COVID strategies, goals, and plans fully integrate the Sustainable Development Goals to create a strong and more resilient world," announced António Guterres, UN Secretary General.

Triple Bottom Line

There is a powerful business case to be made for sustainable leadership. It's not just about doing what's right, although ideally that would already be part of any corporate values statement. Pursuing sustainability goals can lead to greater profitability, as well as stronger morale and increased productivity among stakeholders newly energized by the mission-turned-into-actions. Pharmaceutical giant AstraZeneca, which rolled out its COVID vaccine at cost and prioritized the poorest countries for distribution, received little to no internal pushback from this expensive and high-risk decision because, as chairman Leif Johannson told me, "Most people want to do good. It's human nature."

Corporations can't thrive in a world of poverty, inequality, social unrest, and environmental crisis. Markets will shrink, supply chains will break, consumers and employees will revolt, and external regulators will slap you with punitive fines and operating restrictions. Fully integrating sustainability into your strategy and operations while anchoring it to your company's purpose needs to become standard procedure. This is a question of the legitimacy of your business and a license to operate. But a sustainable mindset goes beyond risk management. It's not just about avoiding fines or burnishing a business reputation. It's the recognition that within these challenges lie opportunities for long-term growth.

My intent here is not to scare you into a more sustainable mindset but to provide evidence of the enormous business advantages to becoming more purposeful about whatever set of economic, social, and governance goals make the most sense and are the most actionable, for you and your organization. Within these challenges lie incredible opportunities. Consider the fact that, in 2017, the Business and Sustainable Development Commission mapped the economic prize available to businesses if SDGs are achieved and identified *$12 trillion* worth of annual market opportunities in food and agriculture, cities, energy and materials, health, and well-being. That's a lot of upside!

Robeco, a Netherlands-based asset management firm, takes the lead among a growing number of institutional investors who are seeing and realizing financial gains through sustainable investments. As of June 2021, the pioneer of sustainable investing had more than 177 billion euros (about $204 billion) in assets that are integrating environmental, social, and governance goals.[8] An early adopter of sustainable investing, having begun quietly in the mid-1990s, sustainability has been at the core of Robeco's investment activities for nearly three decades.

Then Larry Fink, leader of BlackRock, the world's largest asset manager with $9.46 trillion in assets under management as of 2021, grabbed headlines in 2018 when he announced in his CEO letter that businesses must "not only deliver financial performance, but also show how it makes a positive contribution to society," warning BlackRock may stop investing in companies that fail to do the latter.[9] (More on the investor's role later.)

With this rising tide of institutional investors who view sustainability goals as determining factors for their investment dollars, sustainability can become your differentiator in the competition for capital. You will also be in a better position to compete for human capital. As younger generations of talent consider where to build their careers in an extremely tight job market, whether a company is serious about its sustainability goals can be a deal breaker. And a sustainability mindset that's properly embedded across strategy and functions can lead to more innovation, better products, and greater efficiencies in process that will ultimately be seen in the bottom line.

These next chapters will show you exactly how that balance between pragmatism and altruism works in practice. We'll look at leaders who not only have a clear sense of purpose but also can translate their deeply held values into business success. (On a side note, many organizations have different terms for the same goals—ESGs, SDGs, and so on. The realm of sustainability is an alphabet soup of acronyms, but for the purpose of this book, we will use the term SDGs, referencing the United Nations' 17 interlinked goals ranging from ending poverty in all its forms to education access to gender equality to affordable and clean energy.)

We will touch on multiple SDGs throughout this book. But our primary focus is on leadership. If the SDGs are the spokes of the wheel, sustainable leaders are the hub. These individuals have figured out how to embed sustainability within the complex components of their organizations, seeing how all the different dots connect, influence, and affect each other. Sustainable leaders take these values a step further, aligning them with the broader ecosystem of suppliers and customers, society, and the government. They are not just skilled at managing their stakeholders, as any leader should be; they are intellectually curious about who these stakeholders are, how they can benefit from the sustainability goals, and how they can take a more collaborative approach.

Going for Bold

To be clear, this process doesn't always look pretty, nor should it. Many of those we spoke with are leading "hard to abate" businesses, such as bp, and, of course, utility companies such as Duke Energy. But what matters more is that they are taking significant steps, whether that's investing billions in cleaner energy, divesting "dirty" assets, or hiring significantly more diverse candidates for their senior management teams in traditionally male-dominated industries. One could even argue that the changes implemented by these more problematic businesses will have greater impact on the world.

In the coming chapters, you will learn more about the secret sauce of sustainable leaders, such as Henrik Henriksson, who made a bold career switch, from Scania, a 50,000-employee Swedish truck manufacturer, to lead the 50-person startup Green Steel, which is the world's first producer of coal-free steel. And Adidas CEO Kasper Rorsted, who is committed to ending plastic waste in shoe and clothing manufacturing with product lines like the Parley shoe, made from plastic recycled from the ocean. And Ilham Kadri, CEO of chemicals giant Solvay, who launched a culturally transformative diversity, equity, and inclusion program with concrete goals to be met by 2025. Among other things, her sustainability goals include building structured mentorship programs, creating a Code of Integrity, and ensuring fair recruitment, with the target of having a shortlist for all mid- and senior-level openings comprising 50% of underrepresented groups.

These sustainable CEOs commit to solving the problem without knowing the solution. But they can get there because they tend to have strikingly high "LQs"—the humility to learn and the desire to quickly grow and adapt their skillsets—qualities I firmly believe will ultimately determine the winners and losers in this race toward sustainable transformation. These leaders are also willing to commit to a certain direction, even if they don't realize the glory or yield the benefits before the end of their tenure. I am talking about decisions that can have a long-term impact spanning decades. Investment in disruptive innovations takes enormous courage.

Of course, the concept of a purpose-driven business model is nothing new. It has only been since the latter part of the last century, when the primacy of the shareholder and quarterly profit statements took hold, that the notion a company had an ethos fell by the wayside. Kellogg's, for example, was about bringing wellness to the masses before it became a global food manufacturer. More than a century ago, Avon built its business model on the empowerment of women, who gained a degree of economic independence by becoming representatives. More modestly, Milton Hershey founded his chocolate company to make luxury more accessible and affordable and create "moments of goodness." Quaker Oats' early years involved land giveaways and creating livelihoods for its workers.

What's different today is the level of complexity. Blending that commitment and drive for concrete results in a global company where decisions and actions ripple outwards, oftentimes with unintended consequences, isn't easy. Being a sustainable leader takes a unique cocktail of passion, empathy, calculation, vision, and guts. Although it's risky not to make moves toward building a more sustainable business, spending several billions on a fleet of new ships—like Maersk—not even knowing where you're going to find an adequate supply of clean fuel, takes incredible audacity.

You know what to do. Now consider this your invitation to read on and discover exactly how. You can translate your commitment into actual, measurable progress by studying the moves of sustainable leaders such as Duke Energy's Lynn Good, and the dozens of other shining examples I will describe on these next pages.

Here are the rewards when you get it right: as of 2021, Duke Energy decreased carbon dioxide emissions by 44%, sulfur dioxide emissions by 98%, and nitrogen oxide emissions by over 83%. An industry leader in low-carbon intensity, Duke Energy also announced a new goal to achieve net-zero methane emissions from its natural gas distribution business by 2030. In early 2022, the company took additional steps toward action on climate change with the expansion of its 2050 net-zero goals to include Scope 2 and certain Scope 3 emissions. And the regional energy giant continues to oversee the largest coal plant closures in the industry, with a full exit of coal by 2035.

Measurable Milestones

Since 2010, Duke Energy

- **Retired** 56 units at coal-fired power plants, totaling approximately 7,500 megawatts (MW) of capacity

Since 2011, Duke Energy

- **Reduced** water withdrawn for electric generation by 980 billion gallons
- **Cut** approximately 80% of solid waste, diverting nearly 86,000 tons from landfills

As of year-end 2021, Duke Energy

- **Reached** a cumulative, multiyear reduction in customer energy consumption of over 21,000 gigawatt hours (GWh) and a reduction in peak demand of nearly 7,000 MW.[10]

Meanwhile, the company made major strides in renewables, having contracted, owned, or operated 10,500 MW of renewable energy (wind and solar) with plans to increase that amount to 16,000 MW by 2025 and 24,000 by 2030. Duke Energy will also make $600 million in battery storage investments by 2025 and has engaged with solar developers in the Carolinas to fundamentally change the interconnection process in North Carolina and design a breakthrough net-metering framework in South Carolina.

Following the coal ash spill in the Dan River, Duke Energy also achieved a milestone settlement for the recovery effort that will provide immediate and long-term cost benefits for customers over the next decade, resolving the remaining major issues on coal ash management in North Carolina.

I cannot stress enough how epic in size and scope these milestones are for a major utility company that must balance reliable power supply with doing right by the environment. On the face of it, these competing interests could not be more opposed. How did Duke Energy make these strides, and what is that secret sauce that enables a company in one of the most challenged industries to continue building momentum? Again, it comes down to sustainable leadership, which views meeting ESG goals as integral to the success of the company as profit growth.

"Our climate strategy and business strategy are exactly the same," Lynn told me.

> It's not an adjunct; it's not another initiative; it's not something we keep track of on the side. Rather, it is completely integrated with the overall strategy of the company, which is to be a leader in the clean energy transition. So it shows up in day-to-day operations and day-to-day capital deployment. Every investment is reviewed through the lens of how it positions the company to take on more renewables or reduce carbon emissions. So that transition toward sustainability is deeply ingrained in the way we talk about the business, the way we evaluate someone's performance, organizational changes, and the way capital is deployed. It's an approach that's been impactful and powerful for us.

Notice that, when Lynn speaks, she uses the pronoun *we* a lot, and not in the sense of the "royal we." She understands that this transition does not happen without total buy-in of the entire leadership team: the CEO, senior executives, and the board. Although she goes much further, bringing in people with field experience to join in strategy and innovation efforts—an inclusive approach that will be described in more detail in Chapter 6—it's the senior leadership team that owns the success or failure of a sustainability strategy. They alone are uniquely positioned to drive the level of transformation needed to balance sustainability goals with the long-term viability of the business. The ability to inspire is another mark of a true sustainable leader. That passion and commitment must be felt by everyone and become a permanent part of a corporation's culture and identity.

Again, I will drill down in more detail about what that looks like through actions and examples in the chapters to follow. Depending on your industry and the size of the business you are leading, there are many ways to get there. But once you start seeing progress, that feeling of relief, pride, and accomplishment is universal.

As Lynn puts it: "There's a lot of enthusiasm about our clean energy transition because it represents real growth. We can expand the business and feel good about the impact we're having on our communities and the environment. We are now a part of the green movement. This is . . . us."

Sustainable Leadership Takeaways

1. Sustainability is no longer a nice-to-have, it's a must-have, and simply appointing a chief sustainability officer isn't going to cut it. There needs to be a wholesale embrace of value creation at all levels of an organization and across every function.

2. Move up the goalposts. Integrating sustainability into your strategy and operations while anchoring it to your company's purpose must become standard procedure. This is a question of the very legitimacy of your business and a license to operate. Moving mission statements will no longer suffice.

3. Those at the very top own the success and failure of a company's sustainability goals. Who is on the leadership team, and how that leadership team operates together, has the potential to enable or torpedo an organization's progress.

4. A sustainable mindset goes beyond risk management. It's not just about avoiding fines or burnishing a business reputation. It's the recognition that within these challenges lie opportunities for growth over the long term.

(continued)

5. The benefits of sustainable leadership are tangible and intangible:

   a. A sustainability mindset that's translated into strategy and properly embedded across functions can lead to more innovation, better products, and greater efficiencies in process, which will ultimately be seen in the bottom line.

   b. Taking societal impact into account when setting strategy spurs innovation and helps companies to identify new products, services, and business models.

6. It takes multilevel systems thinking. Leaders, and those around them, need to be able to see and understand the complex web of cause and effect across market, social, environmental, and regulatory variables.

7. And it takes stick-to-it-iveness. Sustainable leaders also must be prepared to spearhead true long-termism: making disruptive investments with the courage and resilience to stay the course in the face of setbacks and pressure from short-term-oriented stakeholders.

2

A Shining Example

Never forget: sustainability is about constant progress over perfection.
—Julie Sweet, Chair and CEO, Accenture

YOU WOULD NEVER guess from his ready smile and calm demeanor, but João Paulo Gonçalves Ferreira, CEO of Natura &Co's Latin America division, is feeling the pressure. Since he took on the CEO role at Natura in 2016, the company has been on an acquisition spree, adding iconic global brands The Body Shop, Aesop, and Avon to its portfolio. It's a way not just to scale the business internationally but to disseminate worldwide the sustainable values of its original founders, who've been steadfastly committed to the principles of environmental and social responsibility since Natura opened its first shop in São Paulo in 1970.

Long before João Paulo came on board, Natura's founders—Luiz Seabra, Guilherme Leal, and Pedro Passos—had been passionate about running a business that gives back to people and planet. They set up the company on six founding beliefs, including that the business should focus on forest conservation, waste reduction, climate protection, and using sustainably sourced natural ingredients.

They stayed true to their word. Natura was among the first in the world to pledge to make cruelty-free products with responsible sourcing throughout its entire value chain. It was also one of the first businesses in the beauty industry to offer refills. This was decades before sustainability became a thing, inside a country that's been among the most reckless in the world in terms of environmental damage, against the backdrop of a regulatory framework that appears to be going backwards, and in one of the most polluting industries.

But Natura's multibillion-dollar investing marathon, and the fact that the company has gone public, means the original founders' shares have been diluted. Although the founders still have influence, they no longer manage the company day to day and it now falls on the leadership team to, as João Paulo puts it, "push sustainability deeper into the culture of the company, which perhaps is going to be a bit tougher."

In fact, it looks like a monumental challenge. Being a sustainable company in a domestic market is one thing. Ensuring those principles stick as you grow, expanding your global footprint beyond LATAM nations to North America, Europe, and the Pacific Rim, with three additional iconic global brands, is a whole other story.

Yet maximizing social and environmental results and balancing them with financial performance is "part of my job description," João Paulo told me on the eve of the COP26 climate summit in Glasgow. Not that he doesn't have moments of self-doubt. As he seeks to perpetuate these values through concrete actions and innovations, he wonders about the long-term future: "Is Natura's sustainability sustainable? Can they bake these strategies and practices into the entire global operations enough so that they stick? Can they make sure that every function lives and breathes values like biodiversity, human rights, economic access, inclusion, and gender equality while also driving for profits?"

I believe that, under João Paulo's leadership, they can.

Although João Paulo is reluctant to take credit for what he insists is a collective effort at Natura, that kind of teamwork doesn't happen without great leadership. My own perception is that João Paulo is a deep analytical thinker with long-term vision and ability to predict the future. He is bold, ambitious, and unafraid to explore the many ways Natura's sustainability model can be broadened internally and externally.

He seems to possess exactly the right intellect, skillset, experience, and psychological makeup, at exactly the right time, to lead Natura and its stakeholders to a level of sustainability that is not just net-zero, but net-negative. The actions he's putting into place demonstrate to the world that sustainable transformation is not only possible but scalable and a wholly commercially viable model for his industry.

Under João Paulo, Natura was recognized in 2019 as the 15th most sustainable company in the world by the Corporate Knights Global 100 ranking. It also became the first public company, and the largest, to receive B Corp accreditation, which showcases a firm's relationship with the environment, employees, customers, and community. Its pioneering efforts earned Natura the United Nations' top environmental award, Champions of the Earth, and in 2019 its Carbon Neutral Program won the UN Climate Global Action Award.

Simply put, Natura is considered one of the most sustainable companies on the planet. Yet this sustainable CEO wants to raise the bar even higher. To that end, he has aggressively accelerated the company's sustainability trajectory, achieving much more, much faster.

Courage, Energy, and Purpose

To reach his goals it will take that special yet wholly accessible and replicable alchemy of pragmatism and idealism that João Paulo, and a reassuringly large number of other sustainable leaders, possess.

Although some have questioned whether João Paulo's motives in embedding and implementing Natura's sustainability goals were more to do with carefully crafting a business strategy than a genuine passion for the environment, the two things are not mutually exclusive. It takes someone like João Paulo, who is at once open-minded, cerebral, and dispassionately passionate, to successfully execute on such lofty and ambitious goals.

The Sustainable Mindset

In other words, João Paulo has a way of thinking that is entirely different from the traditional mode of business leadership. He possesses what we call "the sustainable mindset," which encompasses strong personal motivation and an innovative spirit underpinned by a deep sense of purpose. These leaders understand that running a business cannot just be about making money but must also have a positive impact for people and planet. There must be self-awareness and a sense that the enterprise is part of a wider ecosystem. Some are born this way. Others aren't, but something happened to them along the way—a kind of awakening.

At just 26 years old, João Paulo had one of those moments. He leapfrogged ahead of his peers to become the youngest director at the agro-industrial business where he'd started his career. This was his chance to make his mark, and he was excited. He was relocated 600 miles away from his home base to Patos de Minas in Brazil's highlands, where his company had just acquired a factory.

When he arrived, in 1994, João Paulo's heart sank. The area surrounding his factory was an ecological and social disaster. Rich in natural resources, the region was known for its agriculture and mining, which had attracted several industrial manufacturers to the area. The plant assigned to João belched out smoke and poured filthy, contaminated water into a nearby river. The air was thick with the smell of the effluence caused by the production process. The whole place seemed to be coated with grime, and the local population seemed to be suffering disproportionately from various forms of ill health. Anyone with talent and means fled this miniature wasteland at the earliest opportunity.

"It was a factory town in the worst sense," João Paulo told me. "Nobody cared about the place or what should be. It was a part of the operations that our headquarters completely forgot."

The young and ambitious engineer knew he'd been handed the impossible task of turning the operations around and that he had effectively been set up to fail. Walking into that plant every day, seeing what it had wrought on the community, was soul crushing. He could have returned to the more familiar, developed part of Brazil and found a management track job elsewhere. But, once he had seen the impact the manufacturing facility was having on people in this part of Patos de Minas, he couldn't turn away. João Paulo sat down with the other members of his management team and asked, "What are we going to do about this?"

They focused their early efforts on disposing of the manufacturing waste more responsibly. But it still wasn't enough. João Paulo realized that he and his team needed to become a part of the community. They took care of their supply chain, making sure the local farmers were paid fairly and treated with respect. João Paulo and his colleagues even partnered with the local municipality to promote literacy among their workers and offer them a formal education.

"I can still remember the look on their faces when these men and women received their diplomas at their graduation ceremony, with their children in attendance. They had tears in their eyes."

Of course, back then people did not talk about SDGs or wealth and opportunity gaps or carbon footprints. João Paolo, like any decent human being, had been put into a leadership position and realized that he could make a difference, so he simply did what he thought was right.

"I wanted our suppliers, the local church, and the people of that town to look at what we did with pride. And I wanted that feeling to carry on to the next generation and the next."

The contrast between the business João Paulo led back then and the worldwide model of sustainability excellence that is Natura today could not be starker. But it's that mindset, that sense of passion and purpose, that's the common thread, and so much more.

The Four Qualities

As necessary as it is to possess the sustainable mindset, it is not enough. So how do you reach Natura's level of sustainability as a business? How do you ensure that every function lives and breathes values such as biodiversity, human rights, economic access, inclusion, and gender equality while also driving for profits?

The answer, of course, is leadership: a very specific kind of leadership with a set of four distinctive attributes that enables them to not only step back and understand the urgency and scope of the inequities and climate crises we face but also how it applies to their businesses on a granular level.

I alluded to the four elements of sustainable leadership in the Introduction: **multilevel systems thinking, stakeholder inclusion, disruptive innovation,** and **long-term activation.** As a sustainable leader, João Paulo embodies these four key characteristics, along with the sustainable mindset, which I will describe in the following sections.

Multilevel Systems Thinking

What does that look like in practice? Natura's entire approach to the global pandemic was a case in point. João Paulo and his team's solutions for the crisis looked at the needs of the business and the community from multiple angles, restoring revenues while simultaneously taking care of employees, sales reps, the communities in which they operate, and beyond.

Business had been severely disrupted, with 90% of stores closed worldwide and major restrictions on production and distribution. Yet every action step was taken not just to ensure the physical safety of employees and sales reps but also to boost morale while keeping the wheels of the business moving, hiring and ramping up production activity to quickly meet new areas of demand.

Natura &Co's first priority was to help its direct-to-consumer, relationship-driven salesforce—enough people to populate a large city—navigate the situation.

So the group rolled out a "Time to Care" initiative. At the height of the uncertainty, employees were invited to pledge part of their pay on a voluntary basis to help tackle the crisis and ensure continuity of activities. Thanks to Natura &Co's impressive financial results, the group returned the donations at the end of 2020.

The move was good not just for the Natura community but also for business overall. Sales volume increased to the point where Natura had to repurpose a vacant warehouse into a distribution center. Those who could work remotely were sent home, no one was fired, and, again, the leadership went to great lengths to protect factory employees, and swiftly repurposed its manufacturing to increase production by 30% to meet the shifts in consumer demand. The company also offered credit flexibility to the network of consultants and representatives, with payment terms and additional emergency funds. Employees, franchisees, consultants, and representatives also had access to telemedicine, mental health resources, and grief support, and have been encouraged to maintain connections with their colleagues, friends, and family.

Again, João Paulo didn't just come at the problem from one direction. He carefully designed a considered, multilevel approach to a major global threat that spanned various aspects of the business and connected viscerally with stakeholders. Although these extensive measures had the knock-on effect of improving engagement and brand loyalty, internally and externally, they also accelerated the digitization of sales and, above all, the sense of mission.

Stakeholder Inclusion

Although multilevel systems thinking enables leaders to recognize the complex links across the many ecosystems in which their businesses operate, the ability to effectively respond to and actively engage with a wide range of stakeholders is a crucial component in driving transformation.

João Paulo's analytical skills are complemented by a great ability to investigate topics in depth and seek applied learning, which is not common among most CEOs. (In Chapter 5, I will discuss the concept of LQ, or learning quotient. I believe great leaders possess high IQ, EQ [emotional quotient], and LQ.) This sustainable leader cross-references hypotheses to find answers to real problems. He then shares these problems with his network, generating a flow of ideas so that other solutions also reach him. He manages to gain people's trust by making them work not only toward the specific goals but also toward an overall mission and purpose. He persuades through a combination of logic and belief that's so firmly held, his team cannot help but embrace the company's values and support him in building a dream.

In other words, João Paulo does not just manage stakeholders, he includes them. His approach is collaborative, whether that's the sales consultants, employees, customers, investors, government representatives, or members of the community in which Natura operates.

Where João Paulo is concerned, inclusiveness at all levels is a must. On occasion, people have been asked to leave Natura because their approach to sustainability was not connected to the multiple processes of the company.

"This was a big mistake, because that's how you lose rhythm," João Paulo explained. "The throughput drops, but you need distributed intelligence so that every single associate can contribute and be somehow aligned to our goals. When you are too centralized, you lose the edge."

João Paulo casts an even wider net, bringing in external partners from the scientific community and even competing businesses. Natura is part of a global consortium that includes beauty and wellness giants Henkel L'Oréal, Unilever, and LVMH. The idea is to create a "brand-agnostic" and transparent global environmental impact assessment and scoring system for the cosmetics industry. The consortium, which was announced in September 2021, would be voluntary, with members pooling together experience and resources, with results that will be verified by independent, third-party scientists.

"Complex problems cannot be tackled by any single entity," João Paulo explained. "There is a point where we need to collaborate with many different entities at different levels, including competitors who can help us shape regulation at the national level, for instance. These companies have high reach worldwide, so why not work together [regarding] metrics and methodologies?"

Disruptive Innovation

Sustainable leaders also recognize that the level of transformation necessary to make real progress will not happen through incremental progress or improvements to "business as usual." It requires exponential changes to business models and innovation.

Transformation may be easy to talk about, but it is tough to deliver, and it takes courage to challenge traditional approaches. The word *innovation* is too quickly used to describe superficial changes. An aggressive willingness to disrupt the business and the industry, and ask why something could not be done differently, is a must. Sustainable leaders seek out the best available science to move beyond today's best practices toward tomorrow's required practice. They're okay with not having all the answers, and they confidently steer into the unknown. They make bold investments that test the limits of what is possible, with a willingness to cut through the red tape to enable innovation necessary for novel solutions that do away with a trade-off between sustainability and profitability.

Oftentimes, these leaders do not even know how or if they are going to meet these goals. But João Paulo is of the view that setting an ambitious goal can be "an engine for innovation."

"Maybe we're going to get somewhere in between. Nevertheless, we will be ahead of the average of the industry. And that deliberate choice is what differentiates us."

João Paulo and his team have been unafraid to take on environmental challenges that are both risky and controversial, turning them into business opportunities. Take palm oil, for example, a necessary ingredient in beauty and wellness products. But its cultivation can wreak havoc on the soil. Palm plantations require dry land, so palm oil plantations drain the peat from the earth, effectively turning the area into tinder, leading to fires that rage out of control. This not only causes massive deforestation but also releases carbon dioxide. Tropical countries such as Indonesia and Brazil are among the greatest emitters of greenhouse gases because of deforestation, which also endangers many animal species.

So, 14 years ago, Natura set up an agroforestry system to combine the palm oil trees with native and biodiverse forest species. Combining responsible, sustainable farming methods with forest management was a brand-new approach to cultivating a precious resource. It took time and considerable financial investment, but now that the company has proof of concept it plans to dramatically scale.

"We learned that biodiversity is good for the process, the people, and the product," João Paulo told me.

Long-Term Activation

Which brings me to the final facet of sustainable leadership: long-term activation. João Paulo was put into his position precisely because of his bold ambition. Soon after he took the position of CEO, Natura started making international headlines, investing aggressively to acquire those three iconic global brands. They were geographically strategic investments, yes, but the acquisition targets were astute because João Paulo and the wider team recognized some shared values that could complement Natura's sustainability mission. These deals were part of the big picture, where the company saw itself decades into the future.

"We were a mono brand with 95% of its market in Brazil," João Paulo explained. "We decided that we needed to bring in other companies, with sustainability as the filter. When we screened our acquisition targets, there had to be an indication of a desire to generate a positive impact."

Natura's board had been talking about global expansion since 2010. It finally happened in 2013, when the company acquired Aesop. The Australian beauty product manufacturer would give Natura access to its network of branches across Asia. Like Natura, Aesop develops products at the intersection of botanicals and science, with a similar cruelty-free ethos.

Less than a year later, Natura acquired the languishing UK-based brand The Body Shop from L'Oréal for $1.13 billion. The business had 3,000 stores in 60 countries, but it was a risky move despite the geographical advantages the acquisition would bring. The Body Shop's financials were not great and there was some pushback from the board, but it was clear that this pioneering brand of sustainable beauty would be a good fit.

"Listen," João Paulo told them. "We are going to revive [The Body Shop founder] Anita Roddick's spirit."

Everyone raised their hand to vote in favor of the deal.

Next was the purchase of Avon, for $2 billion—Natura's biggest investment yet. By then the company's investment strategy had already proven itself, with Natura's turnover increasing 35% between 2017 and 2018, although this latest deal was risky. The brand's past missteps have been well documented. But employees who remained at the company, despite the setbacks, were passionate and committed. And João Paulo never forgot Avon's founding values.

"They invented this industry and were providing opportunities and empowerment for women 135 years ago, even before women had civil rights in the US, so there was something really special there."

He reminded the Avon leadership of their socially progressive roots. He simply told them, "We want you to do the right thing. We admire your heritage, and we want you to go back to it."

Those words revived their sense of purpose and smoothed the way for the merger. Not that it was simple.

"No one was defending Natura, or Avon or The Body Shop at the expense of the whole," recalled João Paulo. We were joining forces to help each other and the societies in which we were operating. They understood we were walking the talk."

The forced shutdown turned out to be one of the few positives in those dark days of the pandemic. It gave the group some space and time to assimilate that they would not have otherwise had, softening some of the usual edges of post-merger integration.

"When you bring four companies together, it's sort of like an arranged marriage, but this gave us a chance to get to know each other, build trust, and get together."

Of course, it is a long and complicated process. Natura is in the middle of an initiative to reshape the culture of the group as a whole that, at the time of writing, João Paulo predicted would take another 18 to 24 months to complete.

"We need to agree on the basic rules on how to operate, including sustainability."

The public pledge, unveiled in June 2020, lays out the three pillars through which the group will step up its actions to tackle climate crisis, protection of the Amazon, defense of human rights, and promotion of equality and inclusion, setting specific, measurable annual targets to keep it on track.

Three Pillars

Address climate change and protect the Amazon by

Achieving Net Zero carbon emissions by 2030 for its four brands, 20 years ahead of the UN Commitment. Reducing carbon emissions aligned with science-based targets, tracking emissions throughout its entire value chain and that of its suppliers, from extraction of raw ingredients to packaging disposal. The group will aim to contribute to the preservation of three million hectares of the Amazon by 2030, fostering collective efforts to ensure zero deforestation of the Amazon by 2025.

Defend human rights and humankind by

Increasing diversity by 30%, taking into consideration racial or ethnic diversity, sexual diversity and gender identity, the socioeconomically disadvantaged, and the physically and mentally disabled. Going beyond the UN SDG goal of 30% women in leadership positions by increasing its goal to 50% by 2023. Natura &Co will guarantee gender parity and equal pay by 2023 among its entire workforce.

Embrace circularity and regeneration by

Moving toward and beyond a circular economic model to create more than it takes. Ensuring packaging circularity by 2030 and ensuring 100% of its packaging materials are either reusable, recyclable, or compostable. Increasing plastic recycled content to 50% and offsetting the equivalent amount of packaging where recycling infrastructure does not exist to reach 100% responsible disposal of plastics. The group will also instill formula circularity, with the use of 95% renewable ingredients and 95% biodegradable formulas by 2030 across all four brands.[1]

The immense challenge of scaling sustainability on this level, ensuring that the three new enterprises are fully aligned, and that the group stays on track as operations get bigger and more complex, takes up much of his bandwidth as a leader. But João Paulo also understands that, by standing still, Natura risked falling behind.

"A board member once told me that we will be judged 20 years from now by the moral standards of that time, not in the context of the present day. I liked his advice, because it summarized where people should put their attention, and how we should consider things in the long term."

Similar to any chief executive, João Paulo doesn't know how much longer he will remain in his position at Natura—5 years, 10, maybe more? In the scheme of things, CEO tenure is short. But that is not his main concern.

"The longevity of an enterprise depends on the impact it has on society in the present and in the future. How can we be sustainable, forever? How can we keep this going for generations more? These are the questions that keep me up at night."

So, yes, this particular CEO is feeling enormous pressure. Who wouldn't? Yet the fact that he possesses an abundance of the traits of sustainable leadership that we can definitively say lead to success will fuel him daily in his righteous pursuit.

Sustainable Leadership Takeaways

1. Raise the bar for everyone. Set high expectations for performance on a wide range of sustainability goals that include everyone from frontline workers to department heads and C-suite leaders.

2. There should be no separation between the sustainability and commercial sides of the business. Cascade these goals through everything from employee and management compensation to your P&L statement if possible. Nothing

---

(*continued*)

demonstrates the importance of sustainability to your stakeholders than a tangible impact on their pocketbooks.

3. Be willing to listen and engage with those who have different sets of knowledge and experience from you, even if that means partnering with experts outside your business or industry.

4. Always strive to do more. Complacency can't be an option, even if your organization has earned accolades on issues such as diversity and climate, because the problems we face are ever-growing and increasingly complex.

5. Do not think ahead by years. Think multiple generations from now. You will be judged by future norms, not those from the present day, so project as far into the future as you can by the most rigorous standards you can stretch to.

PART

II

Inside the Mind of a Sustainable Leader

3

Born versus Made

Only if we understand, can we care. Only if we care, we will help. Only if we help, we shall be saved.

—Jane Goodall, *British primatologist/anthropologist*

STROLLING WITH HER husband through a crowded bazaar in Essaouira, Morocco, Ilham Kadri was entranced by the colorful silks and spices when two little girls ran past her, practically knocking her off her feet. They were wearing threadbare school uniforms dingy with dust from the streets, their sandals so worn that they might as well have been barefoot. Ilham turned to her husband. "Do you see those two?" she asked him. "That was me when I was little."

Growing up in a humble house on the outskirts of Casablanca, Morocco, in the 1970s, Ilham took nothing for granted. Electricity was intermittent and her home had not been plumbed for potable water throughout much of her early childhood. Daily long, hot showers or baths were unheard of, and whatever came out of a nearby community pump was carefully conserved for cooking and washing up.

"Whenever I see fresh-running water, even now, it's a miracle," Ilham told me.

In fact, all available resources—clothing, cooking utensils, school supplies—were used and reused in that household, where recycling became the natural response to scarcity.

"We lived in a very frugal environment and the conservation of food and water meant a lot at that time," Ilham, CEO of the $12.9 billion Belgian specialty chemicals multinational Solvay, told me. "We were a loving and happy family, so I never felt deprived. Yet we were humble, always knowing that we did not have the luxury to waste anything at home."

A humble childhood shaped her world view early on. So did pollution. At 17, Ilham became severely ill with typhoid, a potentially deadly water-borne disease she believes she contracted from a nearby contaminated water source. The illness landed her in hospital with a raging fever and crippling pain in her muscles and intestines. Her hair fell out, she became rail thin, and at one point her doctors weren't sure she would make it. Ilham's recovery took many months. As her final high school exams loomed, the timing could not have been worse. Excelling academically would be her ticket to a top university—a chance to build a life and career that would enable her to take care of her grandmother, who had spent years supporting her household as a cleaner.

Determined to succeed, she studied from her hospital bed. Against the odds she did much more than just pass her exams. She earned two scholarships to pay for her studies in France, where she studied engineering, chemistry, and physics, ultimately earning a PhD in macromolecular physical chemistry.

The Third Door

Education was everything not just to Ilham but also to her grandmother, who was illiterate. The African-born, Muslim matriarch was determined that her granddaughter had more options than she did growing up in a society that put many limits on women.

"In Morocco there are two doors for a little girl to walk through out of her father's home: one leads to her husband's house, the other to the grave," her grandmother told her. "Find the third door."[1]

Not only did Ilham find it, she walked through it to become one of the most powerful women in international business, making *Fortune* magazine's 2020 list, as well as becoming the first female chair of the

World Business Council for Sustainable Development. She's a member of the steering committee of the influential European Round Table of Industrialists and a permanent member of the World Economic Forum's International Business Council. Ilham has overseen transformations through multiple mergers and acquisitions in the various industries in which she's served: automotive, aerospace, mining, construction, consumer goods, hospitality, and health care.

But it is not the impressive list of titles and responsibilities on Ilham's résumé that stand out to me so much as the way she has consistently balanced the needs for profit and sustainability goals. Sustainability has become inseparable from her leadership role at Solvay, where there is no decoupling of SDGs with business goals. In fact, quite the opposite. In February 2020 she announced the company's sustainability road map, Solvay One Planet, which outlines 10 ambitious yet measurable environmental, social, and natural resource targets to be achieved by 2030.

In addition to reducing Solvay's carbon footprint, including reallocating investments and phasing out coal and soda ash in its plants, Ilham pledges to "tackle resource scarcity and promote a better life." One of her bolder social objectives is to achieve gender parity for mid- and senior-level management by 2035. Another example of progressive action was her move in 2021 to extend and expand Solvay's global maternity leave policy from 14 weeks to 16 weeks, including coparents employed by the company regardless of gender.

Family-Oriented[2]

"When I first told my wife that my paternity leave was extended by 14 weeks, she thought I was joking," said Peihan Shi, an operator at Solvay's specialty polymers site in Changshu, near Shanghai, and whose first son was born in early 2021. Peihan used that free time to take over the housework while his wife took care of the baby. He admitted to feeling concerned at first about being absent from work for such a long time, "but my managers and my team have been very supportive."

(*continued*)

Further north, in China's Shandong province, Ruzi Zhang, who handles alumina sales and technology services, also said his managers and colleagues were "super-supportive" of his decision to take two months off when his second baby came in July 2021. "I'm a salesperson, and I travel almost every week; sometimes I'm only at home for the weekends. I'm quite ashamed that my wife had to shoulder most of the responsibilities to bring up our first son, so the extended paternity was hugely helpful."

There is plenty to unpack from Solvay's One Planet strategy, including the way the business leverages innovation and technology to come up with sustainable solutions and products to accelerate its SDG goals, but more on that later. My point here is that many of the priorities and values of this 150+-year-old global business headquartered in Belgium can be traced back to Ilham's formative years—the very issues of resource scarcity, safety, diversity, education, and opportunity that affected her so viscerally in her youth.

"It's happened again and again in my life and career. I've chosen projects, or projects have chosen me, that relate to people, planet, and profits," Ilham told me. "I've been blessed throughout my career to work for companies that have educated me in that way and allowed me to use my knowledge of science in the service of humanity."

Ilham came into the world with an intense awareness of the fragility of our existence on this earth and a deeply ingrained appreciation for what education and opportunity can do for women and girls. Everything about her early development—deprivation and scarcity combined with an abundance of creativity, love, and compassion—shaped her to become the global role model for sustainable leadership she is today.

■　■　■

Although it may be easy to assume that sustainable leaders have always possessed an innate passion for sustainability, RRA's research has found that is not always true. Sustainable leaders aren't just born, they are made; sometimes they are both. The sustainable leaders we analyzed identified themselves as belonging to one of three categories:

- **The born believers**—those who described a passion for the environment or social issues fostered from an early age, even childhood, as was the case with Ilham
- **The convinced**—those who have come to an increased understanding of the strategic importance of sustainability as they grew into their careers and saw the interconnectivity between corporate decision-making and externalities such as social issues and the environment
- **The awoken**—those who experienced a pivotal moment of realization, prompted by some major event, that there was more to business than profit, and that they personally had to do more

About 45% of the sustainable leaders we studied were born believers, and almost as many, 43%, described themselves as the convinced. The remaining 12% were among the awoken. My own takeaway from these numbers is that you can arrive at a sustainable mindset from virtually any set of life experiences or background. It is something that we can all arrive at through multiple pathways.

Whether convinced, born, or awoken, another interesting differentiator of these sustainable pioneers related to the experiences they had across functions and around the world. Compared with our control group, these leaders were three times more likely to have worked in two or more continents. It would be reasonable, therefore, to assume that leaders with a track record of integrating sustainability into the business have somehow benefited from exposure to multiple cultures, with a more well-rounded understanding of how business works.

"I have been at L'Oréal for 40+ years now and have had the opportunity to work in many countries," noted the cosmetics giant's CEO, Jean-Paul Agon. "This has allowed me to see many different situations and how important the environment and sustainability is all over the globe. I saw this in Europe, Asia, and the United States. It became obvious to me that this was the number-one critical issue of the 21st century."[3]

Experience across functions also contributes to a sustainable awakening. The leaders in our survey were twice as likely than the Fortune 500 control group to have had career experience in two or more roles. Those we interviewed told us that this cross-functional experience gave them a broader perspective on their business and industry, as well as honed their leadership skills.

Notably, most of these leaders had experience in supply chain and operations, where they could see the direct impact of their sustainability strategies on the ground and among workers and what happens when these strategies aren't sustainable enough.

"I like walking through plants and talking to engineers in the frontline," Paula Santilli, CEO of PepsiCo Latin America, told me. "When you are standing in a line seeing the amount of waste coming up—you almost get a heart attack. We understand that there is industrial waste, but our job is to minimize it. We can all read the scorecard; we understand the KPIs. But when you see incorrect usage—the KPI number becomes much clearer."[4]

Although Paula's observation may be more relevant to sectors with production facilities, such as the consumer, industrial, and health-care industries, it suggests that getting out there, walking the floors, coming face-to-face with the realities on the ground, and speaking with external stakeholders throughout the community and at all levels of the supply chain can leave an indelible mark on the mind of a sustainable leader. This is where the education truly begins.

Learning Curve

As Chapter 5 will explore, sustainability requires significant learning at any executive level. Even when people come to a leadership position already having a sustainable mindset and certain specific attributes that propel them into action, they can acquire experiences, training, mentors, and partners who can deepen their awareness. Each role, each project, makes them more effective as strategists and doers. They can continue to take steps that heighten their effectiveness as they navigate the sometimes turbulent waters of transition.

Kate Brandt, chief sustainability officer at Google, is another great example of a sustainable leader who was born that way. A native

Californian, "I grew up in this little town called Muir Beach, which is just north of San Francisco and is named after the environmentalist John Muir. I spent hours going to the beach and playing in the tide pools, and from a very early age developed a deep appreciation of Nature. It's why I do this work."[5]

"This work" has been an illustrious career in the Obama Administration, where she served at the Pentagon as special advisor for energy to the Secretary of the Navy before becoming the first federal chief sustainability officer, where she oversaw the sustainable conversion of 360,000 buildings and 650,000 vehicles.

Yet, Kate shared with me, understanding what needs to be done is one thing; execution is another. Even she experienced a learning curve as she made the transition from the public sector, with all its processes, vast personnel, and clear timelines. Kate compared the inherently limited nature of time in a political administration and the desire to drive as much positive change as possible in a relatively short window to "battling the shot clock in basketball. You can feel the game time ticking and you need to keep going."

That forced timing made people commit to action. This experience was juxtaposed with Google, where Kate began as a "central team of one." Although sustainability has always been in the DNA of the company, with the launch of Google Earth Engine in 2005, commitments to carbon neutrality as early as 2007, and 100 percent renewable in 2012, "there were opportunities to become more organized and strategic across the business." At the time of putting together her first sustainability report for the technology behemoth, she asked her bosses about the direction they wanted to take.

"You tell us," they told her. "Go figure it out."

Initially, without the infrastructure in place, Kate found it was a struggle to get her ambitious projects "out the door," but she learned the Google way, steadily becoming more creative and entrepreneurial in that space.

No sustainable leader, however impeccable the pedigree, bursts into the world fully formed. Sometimes experience follows awareness, sometimes it is the other way around. Either way, they evolve, building on each success and failure, as they should. And whatever the trajectory of their careers, there is always a moment, or series moments, of awakening that changes the way they view the world and their roles and responsibilities within it.

Children's Wisdom

An inflection point came for Mads Nipper, CEO of Denmark's Ørsted, the world's leading offshore wind developer during the early 2000s, while he was in the C-suite at toy manufacturer Lego when he read a letter from a nine-year-old boy in the US who was being bullied by two 11-year-olds on the school bus.

"Lego is for babies!" they told him.

Outraged, the physically smaller and outnumbered child stood up to them, naming all the reasons why Lego wasn't just a toy, but building blocks for the imagination.

"The fact that this little boy would stand up for our brand with such passion really moved me," Mads shared with me.

In the context of Lego, "It dawned on me that there is a much bigger purpose that touches millions of children to a varying extent, which made me realize that this was not just a business."

That realization stayed with Mads when he became CEO of an entirely different business: Danish pump manufacturer Grundfos. When he accepted the position, he looked for meaning and was surprised to discover that 10% of the world's electricity is consumed by pumps. Because Grundfos was the world's leading pump maker, he made the calculation that, through the use of existing technology, Grundfos had the potential to cut that consumption by 1% to 2%.

Mads' second purpose would be to give 2.1 billion people around the world access to clean water by building the world's best pumps. One of the proudest moments of his Grundfos tenure was turning on a freshwater tap in sub-Saharan Africa.

"We are here because water-borne diseases are the biggest killer in the world," he told his stakeholders.

"Doesn't he understand we are just a pump company?" many whispered.

Yet the lessons from those young Lego fans stayed with him: look for something profoundly meaningful, then scale it for maximum impact.

I'll share more about how children and young people are sowing the seeds of conviction at the end of this book, in Chapter 11. Whichever way they come to their awareness as sustainable leaders—whether it creeps up on them quietly yet powerfully or hits them like a thunderbolt—their realization is so powerful, so undeniable, they can never look at their roles in business, society, and the environment the same way again.

Bump in the Night

I guess you could call me one of the awoken. It's not that I was ever dismissive of sustainability. As someone who advises global Fortune 500 companies, delving into their values and needs for forward-thinking leadership, issues such as diversity, equity, and inclusion, and purpose were always a part of the conversation. But I didn't have a deep understanding of sustainability in all its permutations, or a sense of urgency. And, although I have always loved the outdoors, hiking, and logging countless days at sea since childhood, I viewed my love of nature as something entirely separate from my day job. An imperiled environment was not on my professional radar. Then, in July 2015, sailing in the 3,200-mile Rolex-sponsored Transatlantic Challenge, racing against other sailing yachts in a pea-soup fog, something life-altering happened.

We were somewhere off the Isles of Scilly, an archipelago off the southwest coast of Cornwall, England. I was at the wheel in a total fog, no visibility, going 15 knots when, all of a sudden, I saw, a mere 150 yards off the bow, the gray-and-white back of what appeared to be a huge breaching whale—a creature I had encountered in the past.

"Whaaaale!" I screamed, to alert my crew.

Immediately, I shoved the wheel to windward and we cleared by just under 10 feet a floating 40-foot container covered in barnacles on its top. We were so close, you could see its registration number. That container must have been bobbing around in the North Atlantic for 20 years. No wonder it looked like a crusty old humpback!

We'd just had a near-death experience. One of my crew was in tears. I always told my wife the one thing I dreaded at sea most was colliding with one of these things, which we had almost T-boned.

There would be no surviving it. During those jarring seconds, if I'd a clot in any valve of my heart, it had been flushed right through. But our troubles weren't over yet. That sharp turn had us skipping the waves almost perpendicular to the water's surface, like a car skidding on black ice. Going nearly head to wind caused our spinnaker block to explode. It sounded like 10 cannons going off at once. The top of the 14-storey mast shattered into small pieces. We all stood there in shock as this sail cloth with the square footage of a mansion fluttered down in tatters onto the waves. We immediately sent out a warning to all the other boats in the area to alter their course. Then we quickly gathered the sail and continued on our way, coming in a close second in a race we might have otherwise easily won.

That moment, which lasted just a few seconds, taught me a lesson that has stayed with me ever since. I became obsessed with the health of our oceans. I took a deep dive and learned the pollution went way beyond all the plastic waste. We had many tons of steel pieces small and large floating in our seas, much of it the result of negligence by corporations shipping goods all over the world. Something had to be done, beyond individual action; that much was clear. It was, for me, an earth-shattering revelation that finally connected the dots between my professional and personal selves, priming me for that fateful meeting with Lise Kingo in Davos four years later.

The Deep Blue

Thomas Lindegaard Madsen, a captain on the Maersk shipping line and an employee-elected member of the board of directors, knows all too well how polluted our oceans have become. His company's hard push for sustainability through biofuels, changes in procedures, engines, and other technologies resonates on a deeply personal level because of the years he's spent at sea, and the many changes for the worst he has witnessed firsthand: "It evokes feelings in us because we are out there half of our lives," he told me.

Very often we stand and look into the most beautiful deep blue ocean, or out at the vast horizon, just to enjoy the moment. But then we see plastic floating by, even though we are in the middle of the Indian Ocean or the Pacific. Although we've been at sea for five days and are five days' sail from the nearest shore, we can count the plastic bags floating around us. Every few minutes there is something else. It began when I first started my career, but it was rare. Now it's everywhere, and it makes us sailors very sad.

A cloud came over the eyes of this Nordic seafarer as he recalled those scenes. Although the concepts of climate change and carbon emissions are abstractions for most, Captain Madsen faces the evidence daily, and not just in the form of physical waste. This leader and his crew have also been directly confronted with the increasing ferocity and frequency of hurricanes and typhoons. "Clearly something serious is happening." It is why this captain, effectively CEO of his ship, has become one of the convinced.

Those experiences of awakening can be as loud as my exploding spinnaker or as quietly powerful as the shift in perception that Dolf van der Brink, Chairman of the Executive Board and CEO of Heineken NV, experienced, triggered by the death of his father to brain cancer all too soon. His grief led to a period of spiritual discovery and growth that often follows profound loss.

A Deeper Journey

It happened in the last quarter of 2014, when Dolf was president and CEO of Heineken USA based in New York City. He spent months flying back to Holland every weekend to spend those final moments with his father, holding his hand. When he passed, at 66, "It was the saddest thing that happened in my life, but also the most meaningful. I just realized I could not live an imbalanced existence anymore."

The seeds of Dolf's awareness were already there. His father had always lived by a purpose to make the world a tiny bit better—and to work hard at it because it would not happen automatically. Although Dolf majored in business at university in Amsterdam, he shared with me that a second major in philosophy had been his "guilty pleasure." When he first embarked on his career, his focus became "selling a lot of beer and being successful both for my company and for myself." But then, "I wanted to bring the *yin* and *yang* together again. I wanted to call that more philosophical side of me forward at work."

Months later, in 2015, still reeling from his personal loss, Dolf relocated to Mexico, where he was put in charge of Heineken's largest global operations at the time. In his new role, he set out with intention of excelling on traditional financial terms as well as in terms of SDGs.

"It was not just as an either/or, but to raise the bar with the understanding that one bar was no longer enough."

To that end, Dolf reactivated the dormant philosopher within. His was a kind of evolving awareness. He knew what mattered, but he put himself through a process of self-convincing, educating himself on the practical ways he could "mobilize and operationalize" sustainability within the organization. In that period, he joined the Aspen Institute as a Henry Crown Fellow and sought out great minds at MIT. Dolf became a board member of the Academy for Systems Change, a nonprofit focused on systemic change for the advancement of ecological, social, and economic well-being. He got to know well that organization's founder, Peter Senge, and his cofounder, former Nike executive Darcy Winslow, who combined big-picture thinking with practical strategies for building an ecosystem that enables transformation. They helped him to realize that the classical philosophy he studied in his youth could have practical applications.

When Dolf took the helm in Mexico, where he was responsible for 17,000 employees in an operation with $3 billion in revenue and a vast social and environmental footprint, "all those lines converged." In his last operational role before ascending to the C-suite, Dolf had the opportunity to execute a massive proof of concept—demonstrating to himself, his leadership, and his team that it was possible to achieve both sustainability results and financial success.

"I asked myself, how do you bring those additional dimensions into it? How do you operationalize it? How do you mobilize the whole organization around it?"

What followed was "the richest learning period of my career."

During his time in Mexico, Dolf not only convinced himself that sustainability is inseparable from success but he also turned countless team leaders into believers, as well as Heineken's board of directors. His implementation of sustainability strategies in Mexico, where, among many other things, he presided over the brewer's first circular production factory in Meoqui, Chihuahua (with zero waste through recycling or treatment), showed what could be done in its largest green-field brewery planned worldwide. It was that ability to build and execute on a sustainability strategy that was also cost efficient, at the same time galvanizing stakeholders to be more sustainable across functions and throughout the supply chain, that ultimately led to his appointment as CEO in 2020 at the relatively young age of 46.

You cannot be convinced unless you open yourself up to learning. Dolf, like so many sustainable leaders I have met with, did just that. He set himself up to receive a new way of thinking about corporate leadership that doesn't decouple higher purpose from profits. The result is a leader who can effect profound change on a multibillion-dollar global level.

"This whole notion that you show up at work and it is a different place from the one where you are a father or a citizen, is nonsense. It is one and the same. I think we are all starting to wake up and realize that, just as there is only one planet, there is only one life."

Sustainable Leadership Takeaways

1. Listen and learn. You cannot be convinced unless you open yourself up to learning. Many of the sustainable leaders I have met with intentionally surrounded themselves with mentors and individuals with expertise to challenge what they thought they knew. They set themselves up to receive new ways of thinking that don't decouple higher purpose from profits.

(continued)

2. There are multiple pathways to awareness as a sustainable leader, all equally powerful. Some are born, others have a sudden epiphany, many evolve over time. Sustainable leaders aren't just born, they are made; sometimes they are both.

3. Those who develop awareness often have international experience. Leaders with a track record of integrating sustainability into the business have somehow benefited from exposure to multiple cultures, with a more well-rounded understanding of how business works.

4. Cross-functional experience also primes these leaders to think more sustainably. It gives them a broader perspective on their business and industry. Notably, most have had experience in supply chain and operations, where they could see the direct impact on the ground and in the workers of their sustainable strategies.

5. Sometimes experience follows awareness, sometimes it is the other way around. Either way, sustainable leaders must evolve, building on each success and failure.

6. Don't expect a lightning bolt. Those experiences of awakening can be explosive, but they can also be quietly powerful. But the end result is the same: an unmistakable shift in perception.

4

Moonshot Makers

Necessity is the mother of taking chances.

—Mark Twain

IT WAS ONE of those crisp, bright mornings rare for a November in Norway, and you could see the needles on a fir tree from three miles away. The sun shone in a cloudless sky, making the cobalt waters of the Oslo harbor and the sharp outlines of the surrounding Modernist architecture so vivid they almost hurt my jetlagged eyes. With serendipitous timing, I found myself standing in the middle of an excited crowd of onlookers staring past the main dock toward an unusual looking cargo boat. We were about to witness the arrival of the world's first autonomous all-electric ship, commissioned by fertilizer conglomerate Yara International.

The *Yara Birkeland*, as the sky-blue 80-meter-long vessel was named (after Yara's founder, Norwegian scientist Kristian Birkeland), also happened to be the world's first emission-free container ship. It had huge implications for the maritime transport industry, which is responsible for almost 2.5% of total greenhouse gas emissions, producing 1 billion tons of CO_2 annually.[1]

You could not have asked for better conditions for a boat launch. As the *Yara Birkeland* made its way from the port town of Horton some 60 miles to the south, the sea was smooth as glass—a sign, perhaps, that Nature welcomed this disruptive technology-laden boat on her maiden voyage.

So why would Yara International, a fertilizer maker, invest $15 million on an autonomous ship? Why did it make this bold Viking move into the shipping business with a "Tesla of the Seas"—especially when there are still so many obstacles to overcome?

The technology will require a two-year testing phase as it navigates the uncharted waters of maritime law, for which regulations have yet to be written about these self-guiding vessels. Alongside legal liabilities in different territories, Yara International will also have to work out how the vessel will deal with boat traffic in large ports, not to mention the uncertainty of maintaining systems on a crewless ship, which will need to be able to self-diagnose problems and call for human assistance. The project was conceived in 2017, in partnership with shipmaker Vard and GPS specialist firm Kongsberg Maritime, long before anyone knew the Norwegian government would even approve such technology. But they pushed ahead anyway.

Svein Tore Holsether, Yara International's CEO, took his inspiration in part from Elon Musk, the entrepreneur who had suffered plenty of his own setbacks a few years earlier on his path to industry-shifting innovation. As with Tesla's autonomous cars, the technology for Yara's exciting new ship was fraught with controversy. Would whales, seals, or kayakers—the sea's pedestrians—get hit? Could a computer make better decisions on the oceans or at the docks than a human-driven vessel? It was all up for debate.

Yet for Svein, the greater risk was not being on the cutting edge to reduce emissions across the value chain.

"I'd rather be fired for taking too much of a risk and making a mistake than not acting soon enough," Svein told me as we sat down at his sleek, light-filled headquarters, internally landscaped with an array of hearty trees and plants fed by Yara's product. "You have to be at the forefront of things and demonstrate what can be done."

Svein recognizes that big, visible projects such as Yara's autonomous ship enables him to build a story to change perceptions and move the rest of the industry forward. The *Yara Birkeland*, which can carry 103 containers on one trip, is expected to replace the equivalent of 40,000 truck trips each year between the company's fertilizer production facility in Porsgrunn in southern Norway to the northern port of Brevik. It will not only ease the burden on road freight traffic but also cut about 1,000 tons of carbon emissions from diesel-fueled trucks. It will also pave the way for other sectors to take fossil fuels out of the transport equation.

Clean Sailing

Ships worldwide burn 370 million tons of fuel each year and produce 20 million tons of sulfur oxide. Without bold action, maritime traffic will account for almost a fifth of the world's CO_2 emissions by 2050 according to a study by the EU parliament. A single large ship emits as much CO_2 as 70,000 cars, as much nitrogen oxide as 2 million cars, and as much fine dust and carcinogenic particles as 2.5 million cars, according to market researchers at IDTechEx.[2]

But major transformation is coming. So far 19 countries have agreed to support the establishment of at least six zero-emission maritime corridors before 2030. And brands such as Amazon, IKEA, Michelin, Unilever, and Patagonia say they plan to shift all their ocean freight to zero-carbon vessels by 2040.

Yet the new ship will be just one of many innovative ways Yara is attempting to take CO_2 out of the supply chain in what is admittedly a dirty industry. As one of the world's largest producer fertilizers, Yara relies on ammonia. Yet ammonia production represents about 2% of the world's fossil energy consumption—or 1.3% of the world's total greenhouse gas emissions.[3] Svein has committed to remove current emissions and establish the production of new, clean ammonia, which will in turn be converted into green fuel for shipping.

"How can I ask my suppliers and customers to do their part to make our food system more sustainable unless we show that we are doing all we can at our end?" Svein asked.

There is no question that fertilizer is a hard-to-abate industry. Although Yara has reduced carbon emissions from its factories by 45% since 2005, the plant still emits about 16.5 billion tons each year.[4] Svein recalls reactions from peers and friends when he first took over as CEO.

"Instead of congratulations, they asked me, 'Why would you do that?'" he joked.

Smaller yet no less impactful innovations, such as the mobile device that helps farmers make better decisions about when to plant and harvest or the app that tells them hyper-local weather conditions, are answering that question. Or the digital agronomy platform codeveloped by the World Food Program, which, combined with a donation of 40,000 tons of fertilizer, helped 250,000 farmers in Africa triple their yields—enough to feed one million people for a year.[5]

These tangible results gave Svein a taste for what's possible if these actions and technologies could be scaled with full participation from wealthier nations, along with the entire food supply chain. It could do no less than disrupt famine around the globe.

"It makes me very impatient and frustrated when I see that so many agribusinesses still are doing pilots with tiny test plots in the corner of a field. We now need to scale up."

Whether it is inspiring others in the industry to push ahead with their own sustainable agendas or recruiting young talent to develop technology that takes what can and must be done to the next level, as Svein puts it, "you need to build first, talk later."

■ ■ ■

Similar to so many of the sustainable leaders we've researched and interviewed at RRA, Svein is what I call a *moonshotter*. He is among a growing number of top executives who are committing to bold action and disruptive innovation without even necessarily knowing what the exact solution is or how they will get there. They are such strong believers in their sustainability goals that they forge ahead anyway, leading with the faith or determination that whatever piece of the puzzle that is missing will somehow be found. Either through creative problem-solving internally or by reaching out to external partners, they will close the circle of sustainability because this sense of urgency is now so universal that *someone*, *somewhere*, is also working on the problem they are trying to solve.

These daring decision-makers and innovators recognize that the transformation needed to make real progress toward the SDGs will not happen through incremental improvements and adjustments to business as usual. It requires exponential change and business model innovation.

Transformation may be easy to talk about, but it is tough to deliver. Sustainable leaders possess the courage to challenge traditional approaches and a willingness to disrupt their business and industry—they ask why it cannot be done differently. They seek out the best available science to move beyond today's best practice toward tomorrow's required practice. They are comfortable not having all the answers and confidently steer into the unknown. They make daring investments that test the limits of what is possible and cut through bureaucracy to drive the breakthrough innovation that is needed to find novel solutions that do away with a trade-off between profitability and sustainability. It's a kind of entrepreneurialism that, although often the exception in corporate leadership, which has tended to be more circumspect and procedural, must now be the rule.

It would be a wild understatement to say that shipping giant Maersk was shooting for the moon when its chief executive Søren Skou announced its $2 billion investment in 12 full-sized clean containerships with no idea where it would get its green fuel. Given these more carbon-neutral vessels are about 15% more expensive that traditional containerships, had companies like Yara and Ørsted not come forward with solutions, Maersk would have risked losing $250 million by investing in the wrong technology. Yet, as Søren told me, "We felt it was a risk worth taking."

The other unknown was whether the extra fuel costs—more than double the $5 billion a year Maersk was paying at the time of writing—would be covered further down the value chain. Yet the gamble paid off. Since then, then the shipping giant's largest customers, major brands such as Unilever, Amazon, and Ikea, announced that they planned to only use carbon-neutral logistics services by 2040.

"All those problems at the start that we thought were so huge we had no idea how to overcome turned out not to be so insurmountable," said Søren, whose only regret was not telling his board before he announced Maersk's plans to go to net-zero. "I still have the official scars on my back from that."

Big, Hairy Goals

Of course, when I speak of setting audacious targets, I am not describing recklessness. There's always a degree of analysis, research, and calculation in successful risk-taking. But it is underpinned by an understanding that the much greater hazard lies in not swinging for the fences, because when it comes to reaching the world's sustainability goals, there is just too much ground to cover. As Hywel Ball, EY's United Kingdom chair and the United Kingdom & Ireland's regional managing partner, put it, leaders must set "big, hairy, audacious goals" for themselves because the world is changing at such a rate that they can no longer afford to be timid—and with stakeholder expectations so high, "they have to move fast to create the plan to deliver on them."

Since the beginning of the pandemic in 2020, when Hywel took his position, "the acceleration has been phenomenal." Moonshotters may be ahead of the curve, but that curve is rapidly flattening, and those who may have been considered early adopters five years ago now risk falling behind if they hesitate even slightly before they leap.

One of EY's moonshots occurred during those early weeks in the pandemic. Most professional services companies "strip to the bone" during periods of uncertainty, with hiring freezes and layoffs. But Hywel knew how much job security was on the minds of the more than 17,000 people who work at the firm in the UK. Any fallback in hiring could have hurt progress toward its goal for 40% female and 20% ethnic minority representation in their partnership by July 2025. So it was that commitment to diversity, equity, and inclusion, along with the necessity of building trust with EY's internal stakeholders, that drove the leadership to not only protect existing jobs but also continue to aggressively hire university graduates and school leavers, recruiting more than 2,000 in 2020 and 2021.

"You have to be clear about your organization's purpose and make sure that your decisions are true to it."

Hywel and his team also debated whether to access government furlough support and lending facilities to provide a cushion in the likely event of a drop in revenues. There was no playbook for conducting business in the middle of a pandemic, but Hywel was adamant that taking government support would not be true to EY's values and could ultimately hurt the brand, as happened when many other large companies around the world accepted support as smaller businesses struggled—and in some cases continued to post profits.

"You've got to live by your purpose," explained Hywel, whose risk-taking paid off when the business proved so resilient that all new hires soon had plenty of work to keep them busy.

"We were in a strong position when the economy began to bounce back because we made the right calls at the start by allowing our purpose to guide us," Hywel told me.

There is an element of profound optimism among these moonshot makers. But they also need to create an environment that allows for these leaps of faith.

The Maverick Culture

Anand Mahindra, chairman of Indian multinational conglomerate the Mahindra Group, says bold innovation can come from anywhere. The trick as a leader, he explained, is to notice those seedlings of creativity and do all you can to help them grow. The Mumbai-based giant, which operates in more than 100 countries in industries ranging from aerospace to IT and hospitality, has become a global leader in the manufacturing of intrinsically sustainable products, from trucks to waste-to-energy power plants. The company, which the *Wall Street Journal* ranked at 17 out of 5,500 in a list of the most sustainably managed businesses of the world,[6] shifted its entire purpose to products and actions that advance multiple SDGs in every part of the world it operates. It's even using its expertise to help build sustainable cities in emerging markets.

"I wish I could tell you there was some grand plan I hatched, or that our board hatched, but there wasn't," Anand told me when we met, also somewhat serendipitously, at a World Economic Forum roundtable on sustainability in 2020. "The plot I am trying to give to you, Clarke, is that the best things don't happen according to plan. They happen with serendipity. Something seems to start from two or three different points, creating a consensus that we want to be green, and then it multiplies. I am not the chief conspirator. It is really about a spark from somewhere. I can help build it up and then people want to run with it."

It all began in the late 1990s, when one of Mahindra's senior engineers approached him with an idea.

"He told me he didn't want to retire from a company that was known best for putting diesel into the environment. He said he wanted to build an emission-free vehicle before he left and asked for a small budget to get it done."

Anand didn't hesitate. He gave the man the funds. The excited engineer stalled his retirement and traveled to Nepal, where he met with some pioneers in the field, then imported the motors to make a prototype for an electric three-wheeler, or what is called a *tuk tuk* in that part of the world—one of the most common forms of transportation in South Asian cities.

This electric auto rickshaw, considered groundbreaking at the time, was then presented to the government of New Delhi. Mahindra requested permission to set up an ecosystem of dedicated pumps across the city where tuk tuk taxi drivers could swap batteries. The government was supportive—it was one way to clean the fume-choked air of New Delhi's crowded plazas—and started promoting the three-wheelers in various ways until the engines started experiencing mechanical problems and breaking down.

"We ended up dropping the initiative, but it was not seen as a failure," Anand explained. "When I look back, that was probably the first time we went out with a green objective, yet it didn't start with a huge masterplan or written book. It came from a guy with an internal desire, and he was backed by management and given a budget. We advertised it and it became a folklore in the company. The message that went out to staff and the general public was that our company, and more specifically our CEO, believes in a green future."

Mahindra went on to acquire an electric car company to signal that they still intended to be pioneers in this space. It also began making sustainable investments, including a food-waste-to-energy recycling plant in an industrial community on the outskirts of Chennai. Employees at Mahindra's R&D center in that city noticed what an eyesore the piles of garbage had become and asked the CEO for the resources to develop a solution. (By then it was already well understood that Mahindra was all-in on sustainability and innovation.) At the ribbon-cutting ceremony, the government official who was the chief guest urged them, "This is great, but you need to think bigger and make thousands of these in cities across the country."

Anand heard him and Mahindra built nine more waste-to-energy plants, adding several solar and other green energy projects to its profitable portfolio of sustainable projects. These sustainability efforts snowballed when Anand launched the $20.7 billion conglomerate's "Rise to Good" initiative, giving not just a sense of purpose to his 200,000 employees but also strong action plans and funding for sustainable goals such as the education and empowerment of women and girls, upskilling of workers, access to health care, water conservation, recycling, and many more projects that pair societal and environmental good with successful business outcomes.

"It was a sequence of events that made this happen and made this belief system come out. Serendipity is an essential element in what happened and is still happening today," Anand explained.

Although Anand maintains these innovators picked him, and not the other way around, his creation of an open, receptive environment was entirely intentional. He emboldened others with plenty of forethought.

When he greenlit that first electric vehicle project, "it was the most unlikely team ever." Even Anand's executive assistant decided to join this ragtag team of dreamers and innovators.

"The only common ingredient was that they wanted to be a part of something exciting. There was obviously so much passion, but also high levels of commitment. These people were non-conformers. But I truly think you need the most unlikely crew to start these projects."

Although it was admittedly a small project relative to the size of the Mahindra Group's businesses, Anand did everything he could to show them how much he personally supported their dream. He showed a complete openness to their moonshot, which would ultimately lead to a complete shift in the conglomerate's overall focus.

"Your strategy has to support serendipity. We must create an environment—a maverick culture—where all ideas are welcome. As long as their CEO doesn't scoff at them, people feel comfortable coming forward. That excitement is an essential feature of an organization. Honestly, so many of my leaders are annoyingly persistent and passionate. But it's what we need."

When you create the conditions, when you are "chief facilitator", the innovation spills forth. Under Anand's leadership, Mahindra's innovations and investments in all things sustainable have been prescient. All told, businesses, including electric vehicles, renewable energy, shared mobility, micro-irrigation, green buildings, car recycling, and sustainable cities, have reached annual revenues of more than $600 million.[7] (As for the people quotient of Mahindra's triple bottom line, its Project Nanhi Kali has helped educate 310,000 economically disadvantaged girls across India thus far.[8])

"The best sustainability movements come up randomly," observed Anand. "There is something organic about the whole process. But no matter how much bubbles up, if there isn't support at the top, there could be a problem."

Prefab Ambitions

Zhang Yue, founder and chairman of China's Broad Group, waits for no bubbles, relying instead on the sheer force of his own will. This serial inventor just leaps, with more than 300 patents to his name. Over the decades, Zhang Yue has built a multibillion-dollar empire on the faith that he can change the way things have always been done. His push to replace electric-powered air conditioning with his nonelectric version, which is twice as energy efficient, has earned him accolades, including recognition as one of the "World's Top 25 Eco-Innovators" by *Fortune Magazine*, and a "Champions of the Earth" award by the United Nations, where he has served as vice chair of the UN Environment Programme's Sustainable Buildings and Climate Initiative.

"I think the key is to be really visionary and to take a forward-looking view," Zhang told me through a translator on a Zoom call from his headquarters outside the central Chinese city of Changsha. "This goes for enterprises, academia, and government; we will need them all to start solving these problems. The way our social environment has developed means we are always looking at the short term, whether that is for a return or gratification. We need to act on what we see coming; if we wait for it to arrive, it's too late."

By far his greatest ambition is the creation of sustainable buildings, with energy efficiency that is five times greater than conventional construction. To that end, in 2020 the Broad Group developed B-Core, a low-emission core tubular stainless steel technology that is 10 times lighter than standard steel and has more resistance to seismic events such as earthquakes and hurricanes.

On our Zoom call, I was shown a video demonstrating the potential of this material, and it was jaw dropping. These tubular steel slabs could potentially replace reinforced concrete in buildings, roads, and bridges, as well as car and airplane parts. According to Zhang, the super-strong, super-light components could reduce greenhouse gas and pollutant emissions in international construction and transportation sectors by two to five times. It stands to reason, although, because we do not yet have airplanes made of tubular steel, it's hard to confirm his calculations.

Zhang's next grand vision is to build what he calls a "sky city" in Changsha in the form of a 2,750-foot skyscraper (taller than the Burj Khalifa) assembled out of prefabricated, carbon-free tubular steel units that bolt on like Lego blocks. More than just a building, it would be a vertical ecotopia with indoor farms, verdant landscaping, schools, hospitals, and other energy-efficient facilities to cater to 30,000 residents who would be a test case for other sustainable urban communities. But, since he broke ground on the project in 2012, the Chinese government has yet to approve its construction, citing safety considerations—a sore point for this moonshotter. Still, he insists it will happen.

Meanwhile, the Broad Group has already built dozens of lower rise, prefabricated steel tube buildings around Changsha, including a 57-storey mini-sky-city that was assembled in a mere 19 days. Zhang calls his construction projects a living system that can be deconstructed and reassembled at locations and in different configurations, essentially as fully recyclable buildings.

"Construction is one of the most polluting of all industries, but I can make the most environmentally sound buildings for half the price and 10 times the speed of anyone else," Zhang boasted to the *Financial Times*.[9]

The prefab tycoon has since proved his point with the building of a 10-storey apartment block in a little over a day. In construction terms, that is lightning speed.

Playing to Win

There are multiple pathways to bold, disruptive innovation. For outliers such as Zhang, one could argue it comes from sheer singlemindedness. But, for most, these giant leaps forward come from a kind of faith that the solutions will come, either externally or from within. These moonshots are born from decision-making that is deeply rooted in a sense of purpose that everyone in an organization embraces and understands, including board members. And they are propelled by an overriding sense of urgency. No time to deliberate. Get it done!

Kasper Rorsted learned that lesson a couple of years into his tenure as CEO of Adidas. In 2016, when he started with the shoe and sportswear giant, he zeroed in on a shoe that had been developed in partnership with environmental nonprofit Parley for the Oceans. Made from recycled ocean plastic, the sneaker line was small and experimental. It wasn't so much that people within the organization were on the fence with the Parley shoes, but "there was an unspoken assumption that you can't be sustainable and drive for business," Kasper told me. He decided to push hard for product development, marketing, and sales. He made it clear to his teams that Parley was intended to be a star Adidas brand, and resources were dedicated to making it perfect.

At first there were major supply chain issues. Then there were concerns about how the material made from recycled ocean plastic would perform, and murmurs that there was no way to scale this product line. By the time the shoe finally reached store shelves, those problems had been resolved, but there was another roadblock. No one was buying them. In an effort to get to the bottom of why that was,

Kasper himself spent two hours in Adidas' flagship store in Paris asking customers what they thought of Parley. His question was mostly met with blank stares.

"It was clear we'd become too self-absorbed, doing all the right things in terms of production, that we forgot to tell our customers about it," Kasper told me. "We got complacent, failing to think beyond the reusable plastic itself. We were on the right track, but we were too single-minded, and on execution we lost precious time."

Kasper was describing a phenomenon I call being a 100-percenter: when you lose the race because you are trying to get everything exactly right before you launch. Adidas created the perfect sneaker, but their consumer knew nothing about it. His team got so deeply into the weeds of the design and execution that it eclipsed the marketing of the product. They lost passion for the big picture of what Parley was all about, then failed to communicate its message—that all-important market differentiator of depolluting our oceans from plastic—to the rest of the world.

"Internally, over time, you loosen the bonds of what you are doing," Kasper observed.

That's why Kasper turned up the volume on his next target: to make 9 out of 10 of Adidas's products, from running shoes to soccer jerseys, out of reusable materials to end plastic waste by 2025. He intentionally held himself externally accountable because "eventually the world will come and chase you on it." Many within Adidas balked. They were afraid of not meeting this goal, which was understandable, but Kasper believed it was his role as leader to push his team to set all their reservations aside, go hard, and rise to this public declaration.

"Make it simple, make it public, and drive the behavior," he said.

An avid soccer fan and an athlete himself, Kasper naturally resorts to a sports analogy, likening bold and loud target setting to a finish line. There's a chance you might twist your ankle before you get there. Or you don't make it to the end of the race within the time you set for yourself. There is always that risk of failure. But, without that marker at the end of the track, "you have no feeling of winning."

In other words, this moonshotter's strategy is to look at their sustainability goals through the lens of victory. As Kasper put it, "Great athletes don't play to *not* lose, they play to win."

Sustainable Leadership Takeaways

1. Don't fear making mistakes. Greater than the risk of failure is not moving fast enough toward your sustainability goals.

2. Build a powerful story that people can get behind. Leverage big, visible projects to change perceptions and move the rest of the industry forward, faster.

3. Have faith that you will close the circle of sustainability. The sense of urgency for SDGs is now so universal that someone, somewhere, is also working on the problem you are trying to solve.

4. Challenge traditional approaches and be willing to disrupt your business and industry—ask why it cannot be done differently. Seek out the best available science to move beyond today's best practice toward tomorrow's required practice.

5. Cut through bureaucracy to drive the breakthrough innovation needed to find solutions that do away with a trade-off between profitability and sustainability.

6. Don't confuse risk-taking with recklessness. Employ analysis, research, and calculation in your moonshots, underpinned by an understanding that the much greater hazard lies in not going for it.

7. Be the chief facilitator. Create an environment that allows for these leaps of faith, where all ideas are welcome—a maverick culture.

8. Resist being a 100-percenter, when you lose the race because you are trying to get everything perfect before you launch. When you dive too deeply into the weeds you risk losing passion for the big picture. Don't deliberate. Get it done!

5

The Learning Quotient

A failed product innovation does not mean you stop innovating. Just learn from it. Our board told me to keep on the journey. And we did, for years.
— *Kasper Rorsted, CEO of Adidas*

As CEO of the Swedish truck and bus manufacturer Scania, Henrik Henriksson struggled to convince his executive team and board that sustainability should be central to the 130-year-old company's business strategy. Sure, they had made investments in energy-efficiency programs here and there. But Henrik's new, overarching goal had been to make a complete shift to a greener business model.

The company had recently developed a fleet of trucks and buses that could run on biofuels for a 95% reduction of carbon emissions. With the transportation sector contributing almost 30% of greenhouse gas emissions in developed countries like the United States, according to the US Environmental Protection Agency,[1] running large vehicles on green energy would go a long way toward clearing the air and furthering climate goals. The problem was that no one was buying Scania's products, which were more expensive capital investments and costly to operate.

That failure to attract customers was devastating not just because of the financial impact on the company. It was deflating to Scania's internal stakeholders, from the research and development team that had invested so much time and brainpower into the pioneering truck and bus line to the men and women who had assembled it on the plant floor.

"What was really bad was that the news we weren't selling spread across the organization like wildfire," Henrik told me. "The developers were asking, 'Why should we bother doing this stuff?'"

It was also a profound setback because the company, although not necessarily against sustainable transformation, had until then been something of an "old dinosaur." From the time he took over, Henrik had already spent eight months, with dozens of one-on-one sit-downs—shaking hands and looking everyone in the eye to "get alignment." The failure to launch the new truck line risked undoing all that internal negotiation.

The lesson Henrik learned was that he did not go far enough in setting goals or deep enough in cascading the message of what those goals were to internal stakeholders at every level. Instead of thinking about sustainability and profitability incrementally and in the short term, leaders need to set a more sweeping vision and embed that passion for transformation into the entire culture. Only then can you withstand the obstacles, mistakes, or setbacks that are inevitable when you are reaching for something new. As Henrik explained, "You need to use your personal platform as a leader to up your game. You should not go in without a higher ambition. That's what gives you the courage to tweak your business model."

It is the difference between "a sustainable leader who is doing okay, driving change within the company, and one who is doing good for the planet by changing the whole industry."

Powered by this new-found belief, Henrik and his Scania team recovered from their disappointment and adapted. Instead of trying to sell the vehicles directly to their primary customers, like small- to medium-sized transportation companies, they approached their customer's customers—large multinationals who were seeking to redesign their logistics to reduce their CO_2 emissions. They also included a 10-year biofuel contract with the sale of each truck to help logistics and procurement managers overcome their initial reluctance over potential price fluctuations. These moves made Scania's clean energy trucks less of a hard sell to their immediate customer, who became more willing to invest when they saw where Scania's product fit within the entire value chain.

That was in 2018. By May 2020, Scania, which had since shifted its focus on to solutions instead of the products themselves, became the world's first heavy commercial vehicle manufacturer to have its climate targets approved by the Science-Based Targets Initiative, a collaboration among the United Nations Global Compact, the Carbon Disclosure Project, and other international nonprofits focused on science-based climate targets. At the time of writing, Scania was offering the largest portfolio of engines on the market that can run on renewable fuels. It was also launching an extensive fleet of fully electric battery-powered trucks and busses, as well as hybrids. It was also testing electrification solutions such as hydrogen-powered fuel technology. And Scania announced plans to halve carbon emissions from its own operations by 2025.

"My lesson learned was that there was not a proper vision set into the company culture from day one," observed Henrik who, as we will learn in Chapter 10, made certain that would not be the case in his next venture.

■ ■ ■

CEOs are not necessarily paid to have all the answers, nor should they be expected to always be right. Of course, they will make mistakes as they seek solutions to myriad social, environmental, and governance problems we are facing. But what matters more is their ability to learn from those mistakes, quickly correct course, and apply those lessons to future decision-making. They do not just need high IQs and EQs. They must have what is called a high learning quotient, or LQ, which is essentially a person's willingness and ability to learn, adapt, and change. That skillset includes listening, observing, and communicating the often-complex message of transformation.

As a child, your parents may have discussed IQ with you, because it was one of many aptitude tests we used to take in school. Since the new millennium, in the business world, EQ—referring to one's ability to handle people with insight and compassion—has emerged as a valued trait. EQ helps you deal with nuance, enables you to read a room, and adjust accordingly.

But, starting with the financial crisis, then accelerated by the digital transformation, LQ became the distinguishing capability among the many CEOs I helped recruit for leading companies around the globe.

As we face change on multiple fronts, hurtling toward starkly different ways of conducting our lives and businesses, having a high LQ not only affects an organization's ability to adapt; it also determines who is going to stand out among the competition.

On the 50th anniversary of RRA in 2019, at a global meeting in Cannes, I implored our firm to make LQ one of its pillars. As we pivoted our own business, moving from executive search to an increasingly advisory role, I challenged our senior leaders to track and measure how much they were learning.

"Investment in learning is critical. How much are we going to learn to be better at our jobs in two to three years, to move the ball down the field?"

That goes for me just as much as for the people with whom I work. As I write this, I am a 59-year-old chief executive of a global company, yet it is almost as if I am a junior associate again. Sustainability came on my radar in 2015, so in many ways I am starting over in my learning. It does not matter what title I hold. I am the eager kid on his first day of school with his sharpened pencils and notebook laid out neatly on the desk, ready to engage and discover. Every conversation I have with an employee, client, outside expert, or external stakeholder is my opportunity to gain invaluable new insights.

I am on an endless learning curve for multiple subjects. I have never listened harder to my younger colleagues about what diversity means beyond George Floyd, for example. I actively seek their opinion on gender equity or how poverty metrics have been set back since the pandemic. I am also learning more about board governance and activism. I am coming back to the table of learning, right alongside my 30-year-old colleagues, and I urged the rest of our leadership to do the same.

We need to recognize that, no matter how senior we are within our organizations, no matter how long our résumés, most of us are only just embarking on our educations about sustainability. We are far from being fluent in one or more of the SDGs. If we're being honest, until recently these existential issues, though important in the abstract, meant little more than a set of acronyms. But there is nobility in admitting what you don't know. Truly sustainable leaders are humble themselves. They get that we need to look to our younger colleagues to accelerate our own educations as we accelerate their careers in turn—a topic I explore further in Chapter 11.

Change Agent

It's easy to identify the leaders who have LQ and pay attention beyond their own narrow boundaries of certitude. You can tell they are learning and growing because they do not just dig in their heels in response to a crisis, relying on what they already know or doing what worked in the past. Their responses are not reflexive. Rather, they are proactively gathering new information and challenging themselves to do things differently.

A quick example of LQ in action is PepsiCo's Ramon Laguarta, who demonstrated agility in his response to changing consumer habits that were having a negative effect on the food and beverage company's bottom line. Consumers seeking healthier foods and more sustainable packaging could have been viewed as a negative for a company that had been in the business of selling processed, surgery snacks in plastic packaging. But Ramon listened to what the market was telling him. He was open and curious.

The Spaniard pushed hard on both the environmental and health fronts. In 2021, he announced plans to deepen the company's ongoing efforts to cut calories, additives, saturated fats, and sodium from its products. And he made public PepsiCo's ambitious climate targets, which included cutting emissions by more than 40% by the end of 2030, building a more sustainable food system for agriculture and water use, and making all their packing recyclable, compostable, or biodegradable—moves that have been well received by the market. Ramon listened, learned, and adapted. As a result, this sustainable leader has been able to usher in a level of change that turned around the downward trajectory of the business.

The 2020 global pandemic put the need for LQ into full relief for every industry. Executives had to react swiftly to volatile conditions, shifting to remote work settings almost overnight. That moment, along with the demands for social justice and racial equity later that year, truly put leaders' LQ to the test.

Going forward, yet more investors and consumers will want leaders who can be change agents. These top executives must be able to respond to environmental, social, and good governance issues by paying attention to conditions on the ground in real time, using the information they absorb to find solutions for future challenges. There's a kind of elasticity of approach to leaders with high LQ. They can tweak, bend, or even yield where appropriate, pivot when an obstacle requires it, or persist in the face of external pressures, knowing they have done all they can to gather the full breadth of facts, communicate their case, and proceed in confidence.

The good news is that LQ is something you can develop. As CEO, you can find outside mentors, professional consultants, even board members to give you honest feedback about where you can grow personally and professionally. Through the review process and ongoing check-ins with your direct reports, you can actively seek information about obstacles they may be facing to improve efficiency or accelerate the pace of transformation. By regularly engaging with stakeholders, you can keep a pulse on the sustainability issues your customers care about so that you can deliver innovative products and solutions.

The Yellow Zone

And if the answers don't come right away, then pilot, experiment, study. The ability to deal with ambiguity is a competency that is underrated. It's perfectly okay to sit with something, explore, and discuss, as long as you don't dwell in that space for too long. Bold action must always be right behind.

Regis Repko, senior vice president, generation and transmission strategy at Duke Energy, assesses his team leaders on their comfort levels in the green, yellow, and red zones, based on what he learned from one of his developmental opportunities. The green zone has "roles that are laid out, established processes, a playbook for everything," Regis explained.

> If you're operating in the red, you are so overwhelmed by the pace of change that you freeze, fail to respond, or double down on the old ways that are no longer working. But the yellow zone is the sweet spot.

> I always tell folks, don't be afraid to put yourself in the yellow. If you're operating in the green, you're not learning, or at least not to the best of your abilities. If you're in the red, you're paralyzed and you're not learning, either. If you're in the yellow, you have most of it down, but there is a bit of ambiguity, uncertainty, which requires you to be in learning mode. And that is exactly the right place to be.

Leif Valdemar Johansson has spent a large portion of his executive career in the yellow zone—from the CEO of AB Electrolux to president and CEO of Volvo Group and later as nonexecutive chairman of Ericsson to the same role at the British-Swedish biotech giant AstraZeneca. When we spoke, at the height of the pandemic, AstraZeneca was in the middle of a massive global rollout of the COVID-19 vaccine, at cost, to dozens of developing countries that could not otherwise afford the life-saving medicine. It was among the very few drugs giants not taking full advantage of the multibillion-dollar revenue opportunity of the pandemic. Yet AstraZeneca was under intense scrutiny by the media due to some production glitches, clinical trial contradictions, accusations over efficacy and side effects, and gripes about distribution. In effect, the company was caught in the middle of pandemic and Brexit politics,[2] despite the fact that, by delivering a low-cost, accessible, and easy-to-use vaccine, it was just trying "to do the right thing," explained Leif, and AstraZeneca managed to be among the world's largest producers of vaccines.

"With the benefit of hindsight, we could have done even more early work in terms of establishing efficiency in production. We ended up not being able to deliver as fast as we thought we could. And, with the benefit of hindsight, I think we could perhaps have anticipated much more about vaccine nationalism. I am not sure it would have changed much, but, again, with the benefit of hindsight we could have probably used some advice on how politized this could become. I sometimes say that the group of people with the benefit of hindsight is the largest group in the world. And almost anyone can be the chairman of that group.

Yet at no point did Leif and likeminded Pascal Soriot, CEO of AstraZeneca, consider moving away from the philanthropic approach. When the UK government approached AstraZeneca and asked if they could help there was no other answer but yes.

Leif is certainly no stranger to headline-grabbing, world-changing challenges. At Electrolux in the mid-1990s, he presided over a chlorofluorocarbon (CFC) scandal, when it was found that modern refrigerators emitted CFC gases that damaged the atmosphere and burned a hole in the ozone layer. Already aware that CFCs in high concentrations could be harmful, the company had slowly begun to phase out the use of CFCs in its refrigerators,[3] but that wasn't far enough, and it certainly didn't stop Greenpeace from decorating the main entrance of its headquarters in Stockholm with a pile of old fridges.

At first, Leif and his top management were defensive. Despite the brewing public outrage, full information about the impact of CFCs on the planet had not made its way to the top.

"I am ashamed to say, I did not know, and it was not on the Electrolux agenda. We did not think of ourselves as a negatively impactful company."

But there were people internally who *did* know, and to this day Leif blames himself. In fact, throughout our conversation, he references this period and his feeling of shame often. It was a turning point in his approach as a leader; he effectively became a sponge for information and feedback, however uncomfortable.

Study Circle

Leif first created the right conditions so that individuals could feel comfortable bringing tough news directly to him.

"Somehow I was getting filtered information and it was clearly my fault," he told me. "Executives must be able to bear criticism."

His door wide open, he then educated himself on the topic, reading all the books on the environment he could find and seeking scholars to guide him. He even read the views of the late Elinor Ostrom, the first woman to win the Nobel Prize in economics and a pioneer in sustainability and resource management.

"I decided that as a leader, I needed to study the right materials and get to know the right people. I made a habit of getting to know professors of environmental science."

What Leif absorbed from the literature and high-level conversations taught him that the role of a corporation goes far beyond profit-making and job creation.

"That was the point I realized that companies are a part of the society in which they serve."

Leif's newfound awareness of sustainability led him to become more proactive than reactive. Electrolux, then the largest appliance manufacturer in the world, not only replaced its CFC-emitting fridges at short-term financial loss it also developed more energy- and water-efficient appliances such as dishwashers, dryers, and washing machines. And when the chief executive moved on to Volvo soon after, in 1997, he took some radical steps to streamline the struggling automaker. A few years into his tenure the company undertook complete overhaul of its heavy-duty truck line with improvements to safety, fuel efficiency, haulage capacity, and emissions.

"You cannot be quick enough to pick up on what is changing around you," Leif explained.

Orders of Magnitude

Making the right decisions early and getting ahead of your sustainability goals also comes from a willingness to experiment. That means allowing yourself the risk that pilots fail, then learning from those failures. As I discussed in Chapter 4, when you strive to make sure everything is lined up 100% before you leap, you risk falling behind, and there is no time to waste when it comes to sustainability goals.

But Leif thinks in terms of orders of magnitude. That is, he gets enough good data to make a decision, without spending months or years trying to obtain information that is failsafe.

"Saying 'since we don't know exactly, we cannot do anything' is the wrong way of thinking. You don't need to know everything with five-digit accuracy. One or two digits of accuracy is enough to start looking at options."

Leif is also a big believer in experimentation—another form of learning. He gives his people plenty of funding for pilots, with room to fail. He uses the phrase *pattern recognition*—the process of using AI to spot patterns, make predictions, and accelerate accurate conclusions. But you do not necessarily need data analytics to spot trends and make predictions. It is another one of the many benefits of the LQ Leif has honed since his days at Electrolux.

When Leif and I spoke in November 2021, AstraZeneca was in the middle of several major experiments, not least of which was addressing gas insulators in products such as inhalers. Again, from the lesson learned from CFCs almost three decades earlier, when management proposed he recognize that this was the next big thing in his industry for reducing carbon emissions, Leif did not hesitate to invest in solutions. An estimated 392 million people suffer from chronic obstructive pulmonary disease (COPD) globally,[4] a progressive respiratory disease, and 262 million have asthma,[5] with both conditions requiring treatment with pressurized metered-dose inhalers. These devices contribute to the global carbon footprint, so in February 2022, AstraZeneca teamed up with US multi-national conglomerate Honeywell to incorporate a propellant technology that can reduce emissions by as much as 99.9%. All told, it will be an investment of about $1 billion, but if these clinical trials, which look promising, are ultimately successful, it will go a long way toward meeting AstraZeneca's goals of zero carbon across its global operations by end of 2025 and becoming carbon negative across its entire value chain by 2030.

Of course, articulating those targets is not enough, "however bold they may be," Leif noted. "We need not only to be aware, we need to be able, and that most often requires a lot of education."

A Culture of Learning

How do you scale the LQ needed to achieve these bold targets?

Julie Sweet, Chair and CEO of Accenture, firmly believes not just in educating herself but also her entire global management committee.

Because they are in the business of advising clients on how to reach their sustainability goals, it is incumbent on Accenture's team to access and absorb the best and most cutting-edge information available. Although their grasp on diversity, equity, and inclusion was solid, climate change was a relatively new area in which they had to take the lead, "and if it is something that I deem I need myself, I try to build in an education component for everyone," Julie told me.

Waiting for the entire workforce of Accenture to get fully trained and conversant in all things climate would have taken too long, but that top tier needed to at least be able to start the conversation with their direct reports and clients. So when Julie convened that first in-person leadership meeting since the pandemic, in September 2021, she brought in a professor from MIT to speak on climate change for 90 minutes, then invested another hour on the agenda for a group seminar on how this information could be applied to Accenture's client services and internal practices.

Julie, who has a Juris Doctor from Columbia Law School, attributes her educational background and training as a lawyer to her "constant habit of learning." It is why she has been so intentional about creating what she calls "a culture of learning" at Accenture. In her first official video message to employees worldwide, she told them she was creating a learning agenda, with a CEO "learning board" online platform, which made her own training and course work available to everyone. Within six weeks more than 100,000 employees signed up for the online classes.

"I think it is super-powerful as a leader to admit the need to learn, because that is how your people will become learners."[6]

Staying Humble

There is another essential ingredient to LQ that is often overlooked. And it is striking how many successful sustainable leaders I've met— some of the most powerful executives in the world—have it. Humility. Of course, there are exceptions, but by and large the CEOs with whom I've had deep and broad discussions in researching this book have been empathetic, self-aware, self-deprecating, and transparent about what they do and do not know. It is as if they have chosen to be students of sustainability and put themselves in positions to listen, learn, and improve as they drive for results from themselves and their employees. There is a sense in which they are in the learning trenches with their executive teams and general workforce.

Bernard Looney, CEO of energy giant bp, is one such leader. And some might argue that, as one who sits at the top of Big Oil, widely perceived as one of the worst actors in climate chain, he cannot be humble enough. A bp lifer, Bernard ascended to the position in February 2020. He quickly shook things up, avowing an unprecedented transition to cleaner energy; investing billions in solar, wind, and other renewables; installing electrical vehicle charging points at stations around the world; reducing oil and gas output by 40% by 2030; and getting to net-zero carbon emissions by 2050. To these ends, bp wrote off $20 billion worth of assets,[7] and completed a restructuring that brought the percentage of women in top management from 22% to 40%.

"I have a fundamental belief that we won't be around if we simply keep doing what we have been doing," Bernard told me.

Critics remain skeptical, accusing bp of greenwashing, but this sustainable leader makes a point of remaining receptive, no matter how strong the pushback.

"You have to engage, you have to listen," he told me. "You have to be humble. You have to be prepared to learn. You have to have empathy. You have to put yourself in the other person's shoes and understand why they think like they do."

Such dramatic change will naturally result in moments of uncertainty. Bernard was open with his team about what he did not know.

"I will say 10 times a day that I don't know the answer to something. People probably expect me to know, because I am the CEO, but this is a massive business, and there's a lot I don't know. I am human. And if I tried to have all the answers, I'd drive the organization mad having them write me endless briefs on various topics."

Instead, he shadows those in his organization who do know the answers, watching and listening to learn.

"In my mother's wise words, 'God gave you two ears and one mouth. Use them in proportion.'"

Sustainable Leadership Takeaways

1. You are not omniscient. Nor should anyone expect you to be. We are all going to make mistakes as we navigate the complex issues of sustainability. What matters more is your ability to learn from mistakes, quickly correct course, and apply those lessons to future decision-making.

2. Be the new kid. Embark on the endless sustainability learning curve, eager to engage and discover. Every conversation you have with an employee, client, outside expert, or external stakeholder is an opportunity to gain invaluable new insights. There is nobility in admitting what you don't know. Seek out honest feedback about where you can grow.

3. Especially younger associates have something to teach us. In fact, we are leading when we are seeking their input. We need to look to our younger colleagues to accelerate our own educations as we accelerate their careers in turn.

4. Sustainable leaders are not reflexive. They do not just dig in their heels in response to a crisis, relying on what they already know or doing what worked in the past. Rather, they are proactively gathering new information and challenging themselves to do things differently.

5. Be elastic. Tweak, bend, or even yield when appropriate, pivot when an obstacle requires it, or persist in the face of external pressures.

6. Dwell in the yellow zone. If you're operating in the green, you're not necessarily learning. If you're in the red, you're paralyzed and you're not learning, either. If you're in the yellow, you have most of it down, but there is some ambiguity, uncertainty, which requires you to be in learning mode. And that is exactly the right place to be.

(*continued*)

7. Make sure your information is not filtered. Executives must be able to bear criticism and face uncomfortable truths, so cultivate an attitude of complete openness so that the full story flows to the top. Through the review process and ongoing check-ins with your direct reports, actively seek information about the obstacles to sustainable transformation they may be facing.

8. Deal in orders of magnitude. Get enough good data through experiments and pilots (another form of learning) to make a decision without spending months or years trying to obtain information that is failsafe.

9. Share the lessons. Be intentional about creating a culture of learning, either through workshops or online courses. Let the whole organization know what you are reading and studying. Spread the wisdom wealth!

10. Be humble. Sustainable leaders are empathetic, self-aware, self-deprecating, and transparent about what they do and do not know.

PART

III

From Pledge to Practice

6

Weaving It Through

Character may also be called the most effective means of persuasion.

—*Aristotle*

MARCH 7, 2020, just two weeks before the world went into lockdown due to the widespread pandemic, was a day dedicated to the well-being of the women who worked at the head office of Green Delta Insurance Company Limited in Mohakhali, Bangladesh. Their employer was marking the eve of International Women's Day with snacks, drinks, free yoga sessions, gynecological consultations, bone density scans, skin and hair screenings, as well as dental checkups (not necessarily in that order). However, the day's highlight would be a meet-and-greet with inspiring female leaders: fellow countrywomen such as Nasrin Sultana Siddiqua, a wing commander in the Bangladesh Air Force, and Salma Khatun, the only female train driver in the Bangladesh Railway, who were there to share their stories in intimate group chat settings. These activities and interactions were part of the insurer's "Amader Kothaboli" initiative, which translates from Bengali roughly as "the power of our voices." It helped female employees see firsthand that it was indeed possible to break through traditional gender barriers.

"Firsthand interaction and experience sharing of such inspiring women will energize and motivate our female employees," explained Farzanah Chowdhury, managing director & CEO of Green Delta Insurance—the first and youngest female chief executive in Bangladesh insurance—an industry where women are underrepresented not just in South Asia, but worldwide.

Farzanah, who is also a chartered insurer, is a pioneer as she has innovated a way to bring financial autonomy and security to one of the most oppressed populations on the planet. Although Bangladesh ranked 65th out of 156 countries according to the World Economic Forum's latest Global Gender Gap Index 2021,[1] and, officially, Bangladeshi women have educational access and constitutional rights, gender inequality remains pervasive, particularly in rural areas where religious and social customs, such as the dowry system, subject women to all forms of discrimination and abuse.

Farzanah realized this demographic could benefit greatly from financial services but upon launching several products targeted at female customers, she found that demand was far less than she originally anticipated. Social and religious customs mean Bangladeshi women must often seek permission from their husband or other family members even for daily decisions, therein making the journey to financial independence much more arduous. So Farzanah developed Nibedita, an affordable insurance scheme that enables these women to purchase a policy through a specialized app, eliminating the need to visit a brick-and-mortar location with a man by their side.

Beyond traditional insurance coverage, the platform provides resources for women to educate themselves about financial concepts and access health and counseling services. A middle-aged housewife in Jalabari, for example, may have been saving up a percentage of her allowance from her husband for years and need advice on how to save or invest it wisely. As for young, unmarried women, they need access to information about reproductive health which they don't dare ask a family member or male doctor in the village. Nibedita gives her discreet access to all this expertise from a neutral third party. The app even includes a panic button, which sends a customer's GPS location to law enforcement, Green Delta Insurance, and/or designated family members and friends when they feel their personal safety is under threat.[2]

The policy covers perils unique to the conditions of rural Bangladesh, such as snake bites, "road bullying" (physical harassment by men when they are out in public), rape, violence, or even acid attacks, often perpetrated by husbands or family members. (Almost two out of three women who have ever been married in Bangladesh have experienced some form of partner violence in their lifetime, according to a UN Women report.[3]) Before Green Delta Insurance, few insurers in the country openly supported women enduring these traumas because of the social stigma of even raising the subject in a patriarchal society.

"Nibedita is a voice for the voiceless," explained Farzanah. "It's not just selling a product, but a powerful tool which addresses their issues and leads them toward financial and social independence."

So, what does snake bite coverage have to do with free yoga classes back at the Green Delta Insurance head office? Plenty, because sales of policies like these rose when more women were recruited and promoted within the Green Delta Insurance team. Customers who might have been shy about speaking with a male insurance broker often felt more confident speaking with women representatives who could personally relate to their stories. And, female Green Delta Insurance representatives grew to become more passionate about selling a product that would empower other women. That is not to say that male associates didn't share their enthusiasm. But, as Farzanah put it, "Our women customers have forged a unique bond of intimacy with our women workforce."

Farzanah recognized that sustainable development goals need to be embedded and embraced internally before they can be reached externally. The insurance products for women were met not only with resistance from customers when she first launched them but also from her board. Her male-dominated leadership team wasn't getting it either. So, she banded the few female managers and executives who worked at Green Delta Insurance, coalescing them around the purpose of Nibedita and the empowerment of women. Farzanah then set about aggressively hiring associates from other industries, seeking diverse candidates of character who didn't necessarily have direct experience in the finance or insurance sectors.

"I tried to figure out who are the people who have heart and want to make it work."

She reached out at the university level, setting up "innovation cells" to attract multigenerational talents. She conducted town halls and set up online portals for training. She searched for candidates with "empathy and emotional intelligence" who "wanted to improve" and understood that success was "about helping people *and* generating revenue."

The result was a profound shift in the internal culture of Green Delta Insurance. Seeing the positive business results of Farzanah's drive for gender equality and diversity, more men within the organization got behind the products, which included policies for other marginalized members of Bangladesh society such as small-business owners and farmers. One old-school male broker later admitted to Farzanah that, for three years, he did not understand the SDGs, "so he just followed instructions." But, as he began meeting and interacting one on one with stakeholders like the Nibedita policy holders, witnessing firsthand how growth and inclusiveness are interwoven, "he gets it."

■ ■ ■

It's one thing to announce your commitment to sustainability as a leader and quite another to embed that purpose into the entire framework of an organization, where it needs to be believed in and embraced by all your stakeholders. But sustainable leaders must do both. They need the drive and the discipline to transform the way their organization operates, internally and externally, as well as through the supply chain.

Ultimately, you cannot get real, measurable results until you bring others along. That means everyone from plant workers to customers to shareholders are galvanized and inspired to embrace and act on their SDGs. When you cascade the mission mindset, bringing about the innovation and flexibility it takes to change the way things have always been done, sustainability becomes everyone's passion and problem to solve.

As Alan Jope, CEO of Unilever, explained, "Sustainable business isn't a strategic priority. It is our strategy."[4]

To that end, the consumer giant created the "Unilever Compass"— a clearly stated intention to show that sustainable business drives superior performance.

"The Compass defines everything we do," Alan said. "The priorities we set. The investments we make. The people we look for. The businesses we acquire. In other words, it is a truly integrated and embedded approach—a red thread that runs throughout the whole company."

Unilever's Compass serves as a kind of framework for delivery in expanding layers, spurring action through different spheres of influence. As Alan explained:

- It starts with our operations and workforce, putting our own house in order, including importantly, engaging employees, and connecting the company's objectives to their personal sense of purpose.
- Next is the value chain, using our size and scale for influence with suppliers and customers to improve livelihoods on everything from sustainable sourcing to living wages.
- Our brands represent the next layer, using the power of consumer connections to change behaviors in a way that has a lasting and meaningful positive social and environmental impact.
- And finally, the wider societies in which we operate, using collaboration, partnerships, and advocacy to change systems in order to deliver on agendas key to us, or to one of our brands.[5]

From Jungle to Store Shelf

As discussed in Chapter 2, Brazilian beauty company Natura has embedded biodiversity into every level of its supply chain. It uses only fair trade ingredients from the local communities within the rainforest, sending teams of scientists into remote areas to learn about biodiverse indigenous components. The process is long, painstaking, and multifarious but, as CEO João Paulo describes it, well worth the investment:

Many of these communities take 5 to 10 days to reach by boat. Anthropologists go there first to talk with the locals and learn their habits. Then researchers come to study the

(*continued*)

plants, their fruits, and seeds, which can sometimes take as many as 15 years to understand how to extract their active ingredients. These scientists then use leading-edge technology to formulate these raw materials into high-performing cosmetics. Then Natura's sales and marketing team communicate to the customer, who pays a premium to participate in a cycle, knowing that part of the profit not only goes back to the community to pay for the ingredients, but the knowledge and access to their genetic contents. Later on, we add carbon compensation projects into those communities.[6]

It means that the people of the Amazon, who once earned a subsistence living by selling the fruits of the forest for a pittance, stripping their local environment to survive, have been incentivized to preserve its treasures and are well compensated to participate in Natura's conservation efforts. They've become critical stakeholders within the company's sustainable ecosystem.

The Perception Gap

Sustainability must be embodied before it can be embedded, much less cascaded outward to the rest of the world. Yet in our research at RRA we were struck by a gap in perceptions between leaders and their employees, or what we call the say/do divide. We found a big difference between what leaders say they are doing on sustainability on what employees see them do.

Although 43% of C-suite executives say their organization has a sustainability strategy that has been acted on and clearly communicated, just 29% of employees agree. And, although 51% of C-suite executives say their CEO is personally committed to advancing sustainability and organizational progress has been made, just 26% of employees say the same. Finally, although 78% of C-suite executives say their organization is doing all it can to reduce its impact on climate change, only 53% of employees say the same.

Take the Quiz

Audit your sustainability strategy, with a specific focus on distinguishing between surface-level or short-term actions and deep investments in changing organizational operating procedures and business models. Determine the level of understanding of, and buy-in for, your sustainability strategy across multiple levels within the organization. Leverage areas of skepticism as opportunities to sharpen your plans. Ask yourself these questions:

- How engaged and involved are our employees and the community in our strategy?
- How effectively have we connected (and communicated) employee priorities into the priorities of the organization?
- Are we effectively leveraging the diversity of vantage points on problems and opportunities that employees and communities can provide?

A pervasive problem that is contributing to this perception divide is the fact that so many C-suite leaders—those who arguably have the inside track on what is really happening—see sustainability as a branding exercise or reputational issue. In fact, 45% of C-suite leaders we spoke with were candid in saying brand management was the driving force behind their sustainability actions—that is, they wanted to be seen as socially responsible or reputable. By comparison, just 21% said value creation set the agenda.

To be sure, the message to the marketplace matters. But organizations that are motivated first and foremost by brand management concerns are less likely to make lasting changes toward sustainable business. And let's not forget that employees are astute. They know the difference between authentic and inauthentic action. A brand-first strategy is a risky proposition that will do little to engage employees—and could lead to accusations of greenwashing. Surface-level actions will not deliver real gains in sustainability. Ultimately, when leaders look at sustainability through the lens of value creation and impact reduction, they are better placed to identify the actions needed to integrate sustainability across business strategy. If leaders are to make tangible progress toward their sustainability goals, they must first commit to making deep changes to their business strategy and operations.

Into the Heart

So how do you bring employees along?

Of course, the embedding process starts with the leadership team. Driving sustainability transformation is, at its core, about the lens through which decisions are made—and this lens is a direct result of the priorities, perspectives, and passions of the leaders steering the organization. Who is on the leadership team and how that leadership team operates together have the potential to enable or torpedo an organization's progress on sustainability.

After all, employees want to work for companies with a clear purpose—and they look for leaders who not only take a stand but also match what they say they will do with meaningful, measurable, and consistent actions.

We know that, for many leaders, this doesn't come easily. In our research, only 31% of employees say the senior leaders at their organization lead by example. This is unlikely to simply be a problem of perception—even respondents who are part of the leadership team do not typically see this attribute in their senior executives either.

Leadership is always on display, and executives are increasingly challenged to lead more authentically and transparently. How would you measure up—and would your employees agree?

Walking the Talk

Leadership acumen is essential, but so too is building an authentic culture of sustainability that runs from the top of the organization all the way to the frontline.

To that end, a crucial first step is to look at your own performance on diversity, equity, and inclusion (DE&I), as Farzanah did at Green Delta Insurance. DE&I should be a critical focus for every business—as a sustainability goal in its own right and as a bellwether for the health of the organization. Those who are failing on diversity are at a talent disadvantage. Lack of diversity not only blunts the skill capital an organization needs to make advances on other sustainability goals but also it means that it is unlikely to have the engagement capital needed to power the change and initiatives that sustainability requires.

Introduced in Chapter 3, Maersk Captain Thomas Lindegaard Madsen, who has been openly gay throughout his 30-year career at the helm of container ships, views his employer's overall strides toward climate goals in lockstep with its progressiveness on LGBTQ rights. Captain Madsen, who is also an employee-elected member of the board of directors at Maersk, always felt relatively supported, or at least not excluded, as a captain with oversight over hundreds of crew members from all parts of the world.

"Maybe it's because we fly the Danish flag, with Danish culture as the backbone, and I am an officer in charge, but I've never had any bad experiences. And I've had the powerful backup of my company."

But he did not exactly feel embraced.

"It was more of a don't ask, don't tell situation."

Management simply did not want to know. For years, he asked his onshore superiors if they would show their support for Gay Pride in Copenhagen, and the response was a deflating, "No, no, no, the time is not right," the master mariner shared with me.

Captain Madsen, who fell in love with and married his chief officer, is loud and proud, and, with his close-cropped beard, dazzling smile, and Viking physique, is something of a social media celebrity in Denmark. He wanted more from his employer than silent acceptance. This offshore/ onshore leader wanted other LGBTQ colleagues, particularly those who did not have his rank and power, to feel free to be their authentic selves. Being represented in the parade would send a strong message throughout Maersk, from the ship's deck crew to staff on the loading docks.

"Behind the scenes I drank so many cups of coffee with so many people, trying to get them to understand that the only way we can attract and keep the best talent, the only way we could develop and transform our company, was to be diverse and inclusive."

Finally, in 2018, Maersk's senior leadership relented, and Maersk participated in its first Copenhagen Pride. In 2021, Maersk introduced its first rainbow-colored containers—"rainboxes"—sending a strong public signal promoting DE&I. The shipping giant has since sent these containers around the world and given their employees in different ports the opportunity to sign their interiors with personal pledges.

The initiative was a hit internally at Maersk, Captain Madsen told me, "all the way up to the management team and the board of directors, who have now seen the light that people who can be themselves work harder and come up with better ideas." The very same senior colleagues who were reluctant are now so on board that some of his LGBTQ colleagues joked by the end of that summer "it's maybe a little too much color of the rainbow for us."

As one who, as he put it, could be "drinking coffee in the engine room with his crew in morning, then dining at a fine restaurant with his fellow board members in Copenhagen by the evening," the captain has unique insight on how to build a culture that can drive sustainability. Whether it is using green fuel such as methanol to run his ship or attracting the best talent for the future of the company, he sees from below deck to the C-suite how it all connects.

On the Front Line

Identifying those on the front lines with the potential to lead change is a smart strategy of embedding sustainability—and one that Duke Energy CEO Lynn Good, whom you met in Chapter 1, used when she tapped Regis Repko for the position of senior vice president, generation and transmission strategy. Lynn wanted someone who not only understood the top leadership's sustainability goals and embraced their purpose but also had risen through various roles on the front lines. Ideally, this candidate would be someone in whom other employees at the company could see themselves.

Regis, an engineer by training, had spent more than 30 years in various hands-on roles in the nuclear energy division before becoming chief fossil-hydro officer in 2016, so he had a depth and breadth of experience that would be an asset as Duke Energy embarked on its ambitious transition to cleaner energy. But he knew it would be a daunting task so when Lynn called him he didn't say yes right away. Instead, he "mapped out" what would be required to make the vast cultural and operational shift (multilevel systems thinking), carefully listing whom he could bring along with him, and how.

"I've said that every plant is made up of pipes, pumps, valves, and water. What makes the difference is the people: their level of engagement, their technical aptitudes, knowledge, experience, and training," Regis told me, just months into his new role.

It began, of course, with handpicking his own leadership team to help him articulate the vision and execute, engaging and bringing others along through showing, metrics, rather than telling.

"I was up-front with them," Regis recalled. "I told them nothing about this would be easy, and it would be full of challenges and not without controversy. I asked them, 'Are you in or are you out?' They were all-in."

These were subject experts who could advocate and articulate solutions, but they also had to have the right mindset: "Whether its sustainability or something else, it's about building a workforce that can make a change," Regis told me. "They need the same characteristics, like someone who is willing to challenge the status quo, who is more interested in how something can be done versus how it used to be done. Someone who can catalyze a team of people to go after a big complex assignment without necessarily knowing what the answer will be at the end. They make progress along the way, stop early when it looks like failure, but have the resilience to keep going with something new."

But equally important to Duke Energy's ability to embed its sustainability principles was a ground-up approach. Retiring old facilities and building new ones, all the while keeping the lights on and maintaining safety and reliability for a dangerous yet life-and-death product, would have a major impact on the lives and livelihoods of Duke Energy's stakeholders. The key concern, of course, was job security in the face of plant closures. Other lifers at Duke Energy were understandably nervous. If Regis was going to face pushback, it would come from that fear.

"People were worried about mortgage and car payments, and whether their next positions would even exist in five years."

Yet he and his team managed to find positions for most of the employees if they were open to retraining and/or relocation. The trick was his deep understanding of how their existing skills could transfer. He thought through a new management system and pay grade for future jobs, offering training and upskilling for those interested in a transfer of roles.

Of course, people left. During times of transition, attrition is inevitable. But Regis and the team he assembled inspired confidence in their workforce that there was a future for them in a more sustainable function if they were flexible and open to learning. Once these associates can see their future at a different kind of energy company, they are as fully committed to their organization's sustainability goals as the C-suite executive whose bonus package is tied to its metrics.

"We had numerous examples where folks got out of their box to really demonstrate their capabilities," Regis told me. "And that is what we conveyed to them: the more you can demonstrate your adaptability, particularly through multiskilling, we will keep these doors across the enterprise open to you for a career path in Duke Energy."

A case in point: a mechanic from a coal plant applied to work as an outage manager at one of Duke Energy's hydro facilities in the Western Carolina mountains.

"With all due respect, what do you know about hydro facilities?" Regis asked him.

"I'm a qualified advanced rigger and lifter," the man told him. "The biggest risk to outages is lifting and moving these machines, whatever type of plant it is. Besides, mechanical or electrical, I know good work when I see it."

And with that, Regis shook his hand and welcomed the coal plant mechanic to his new green energy workplace.

The Authenticity Test

Hiring for a sustainable mindset, at all levels of the organization, is another way to weave it through. Peter Vanacker, CEO of Lyondell-Basell, one of the largest plastics, chemicals, and refining companies in the world, and former CEO and president of Neste Corp., has always been a stickler for character. He seeks candidates who possess agility, approachability, and transparency alongside strategic and execution skills.

"You need to consider whether people have balanced egos; if they listen to what others say and can take others seriously; if they work in a diverse environment in an agile and flexible way," Peter explained. "Balanced egos help because it means people are willing to learn."

Aligning company purpose with the hiring process must go beyond roles, responsibilities, and skillsets to psychometrics. At Neste, Peter considered whether candidates spoke with passion when they talked about sustainability and company purpose. They were asked detailed questions around the subject and given scenarios to see how they reacted and what they would do.

"It was so critical for us, that if we thought the person is skilled but not authentic, we would not hire them," Peter told me.

Once inside the organization, online training around sustainability was required of all employees. Although the test results were confidential, employees who failed the test needed to take it again, and everyone underwent approximately 24 hours of training "on the environment, health, safety, footprint, and handprint of Neste's operation."

There were no exceptions to this rule. In 2019, Neste hired 1,200 people and, for every position, this passion for sustainability was part of the job description. Once inside the organization, everyone was included in the embedding process. At least 50% of the entire workforce provided input as Neste reframed its purpose from "to *leave* a healthier planet for the next generation," to "creating a healthier planet for our children." And all employees had a say in developing values around the concept of courage.

"We couldn't just have it for leaders and office jobs," explained this sustainable leader, who in mid-2022 assumed his new role as chief executive of LyondellBasell. "It's about the heart and conviction that people have."

Training, engagement, and inclusion are key to cascading the message and ensuring it is embraced at all levels of the organization. Helping stakeholders see why it should matter to them on a micro level, giving them a sense of individual purpose—a direct role in furthering the sustainability goals—and recognizing those who have taken initiative by innovating or exceeding targets: these are all ways that successful leaders have embedded the SDGs, ensuring they are much more than some top-down edict or superficial branding effort. Sustainable leaders understand that authentic employee engagement is central to their communications and engagement strategies. They take a deep scan of how connected employees are to the organization's purpose and whether they are manifesting the right behaviors and values and leverage their diversity of perspectives across functions.

Writer's Cramp

About a year into his tenure as CEO of fertilizer giant Yara, Svein Tore Halsether decided it was time to write a book that retold the company's story in the context of sustainability. The point was to build a sense of pride in Yara's history through stories like the fact that its founder was the first to extract nitrogen from the air to produce fertilizer, helping to avoid famine in Europe and saving millions of lives. The booklet also outlined a way forward and made clear the company's overall purpose. Svein then chose to personally sign each copy, shaking the hand of each recipient during dozens of town halls around the world.

"I failed to do the mathematics of how long it takes to sign 17,000 books."

But the personal touch did the trick.

"Now anyone from a plant operator in South Africa to a country manager in Vietnam knows the purpose that drives our company."

The Art of the Possible

Accenture is one professional services company that has made the embedding of sustainability central not just to its own business strategy but also to the thousands of organizations around the globe that are among its clients.

I first met Julie Sweet, the company's chair and chief executive officer, on a bright and sunny day at Davos in 2020, when the Decade of Action on sustainability was launched. This was a significant moment in the world's sustainability journey because we were already 20 years into the SDGs, and nowhere near enough progress had been made. It was decided that the 10,000 corporate cosignatories to the UN Global Compact needed to be held accountable for promises long since made, with measurable results. Julie was a big part of that serious conversation. She was seated next to UN Secretary General António Gutierrez, and my place at the table was next to her (quite the turnaround from my first snowy visit 12 months earlier).

What struck me about this leader during that and many subsequent meetings was her thoughtfulness, clarity, and focus. Julie had a way of articulating the business case and existential urgency of sustainability that was at once overarching and laser-focused on detail. A year later, she made headlines when she announced that sustainability was the new digital, and that a "twin transformation" through digital and sustainability was critical for business success, and, as with digital, reskilling employees to achieve the SDGs was a key component of this transformation.

By September 2019, when she took her global CEO position, Accenture was already far along in its inclusion, diversity, and equity journey. Julie immediately asked herself if they were doing enough. After all, their core business was now offering consulting services and technological solutions to help most major corporations around the world reach their climate goals and offer metrics to keep them transparent and on track, so it made sense for the firm to infuse the behavior they were urging in other organizations across their own business functions.

"Your organization can't be a leader helping your clients unless you are leading yourself," Julie told me.

Julie challenged her team to think boldly about how to get to net zero, and not use a path that was mainly buying credits, as they had seen many others do. She then asked her extended leadership team to think about where the possible intersected with the business value proposition. Accenture was already a global leader in digitization, accelerated by the pandemic lockdowns, and demand for sustainable solutions for functions such as cloud computing, for example, was growing exponentially. There was a clear business opportunity to "go big in sustainability services." Not least, it was a way to attract and retain talent, "because we know what the people who are performing care about." The result was a decision not only to commit to net zero for Accenture by 2025 and continue to grow sustainability services, but also to seek ways to embed sustainability across the work it does for clients, regardless of whether it would be a separate service.

Getting everyone to not just embrace but also *act* on these sustainability goals would require a system of accountability. Julie added sustainability as a category on a "shared success scorecard" for the 500 top leaders who are innovating and driving the business. Their performance is being measured by whether the company as a whole is achieving its goals for climate change, upskilling, community work, and other evolving strategic priorities.

Accenture also created a priority-setting framework for its 9,000 managing directors. Beyond the usual performance benchmarks such as sales and revenue, each will have to choose two personal priorities: inclusion, diversity, and equity (a non-negotiable) and an array of sustainability goals from pandemic relief to recycling. Their performance would then be measured by the bar they set for themselves.

"It shows our leaders that these things all matter," Julie explained.

The net effect: sustainability is embedded across every function. Its priorities have scaled, touching all the company's people in offices and operations, 200 cities across 50 countries. To drive home that point, and "in recognition of what matters to them," Julie had a tree planted for each of Accenture's then-674,000 people. That same week in December 2021 this was announced, Accenture delivered very strong results for its first quarter of fiscal year 2022, with revenues of $15.0 billion, an increase of 27%, earnings per share of $2.78, a 20% increase, and record new bookings of $16.8 billion, a 30% increase, from the first quarter of 2021.[7]

Coincidence? I don't think so.

Sustainable Leadership Takeaways

1. Update selection frameworks to measure individuals' sustainable leadership track record. Enable the board and senior management to apply sustainability as a key criterion when selecting and promoting leaders.

2. Integrate sustainability into the objectives, incentives, and remuneration of the CEO and executive team. Reward and promote those who lead sustainably.

3. Make long-term disruptive investments in talent, leadership, and culture. Consider creating new positions or functions, elevating existing mandates, or investing in new tools to support sustainable transformation.

4. Take a candid view of your leadership team's perceptions of sustainability. Identify issues that may contribute to an unwillingness or inability to make it a core strategic objective, such as deference to hierarchy, risk aversion, being stuck in the past.

5. Consider whether your executive team has the soft skills needed to manage diverse stakeholders, bridge divides between groups, and motivate employees to engage in a change journey.

6. Push hard on DE&I, with a specific focus on defining concrete actions (not just goals) for improving diversity at senior levels within the organization.

7. Get specific. Translate enterprise-wide sustainability goals into concrete actions and measurable objectives that leaders and employees alike can feel in their day-to-day work.

7

From CSO to CEO

Out of the sighs of one generation are kneaded the hopes of the next.
—Machado de Assis, 19th-century Brazilian novelist/poet/playwright

WALKING FACTORY LINES to survey conditions was a big part of the job for Sophia Mendelsohn. The young executive traveled all over China on behalf of major brands to balance speed, quality, and global safety standards at manufacturing facilities. Air quality issues, waste and discharge, and even metal shavings were par for the course on these fact-finding missions that took her to the remote corners of the mainland, to factory towns that had often sprung up solely for the sake of producing goods as efficiently as possible, first for export and later for national consumption.

Walking through one factory, Sophia gathered information the way she always did when she was on site: by chatting to the people on the front lines in her fluent Mandarin. Through these conversations she learned about the process of manufacturing: the production line, efficiency or waste, the need for speed, and the motivations of the workers and managers. But never was an answer so stark as when she struck up a conversation with one local resident and asked him how his life had changed during the previous decade.

"I wouldn't give up the money and progress for the world," he told her, referring to not only his personal salary but also the general economic uplift in his community and country. "But it's heartbreaking to see the negative consequences of development right here in my own community."

It was an emotional moment for Sophia, who now serves as chief sustainability officer and head of ESG for Cognizant, a Fortune 200 information technology and services provider. The worker wasn't complaining or casting blame, she recalls. Nor was he exaggerating the health and environmental effects that China—or any country—takes on when they become a manufacturing hub for the world. He was simply telling the truth about the trade-off of economic progress.

That conversation was one of many crossroads in Sophia's career as a sustainable leader. In the early 2000s, part of her job was to bridge the divide between global cultural differences and the pressures manufacturers and retailers felt to provide goods as quickly and cheaply as possible, with seemingly no change in quality or design.

"At that time, there was a true tension between a US company's desire to import their progressive environmental health and safety standards to their supply chain and the reality that many companies had sensitized their China-based manufacturing partners to the lowest production price point possible," Sophia told me, more than a decade later. "And those two realities were coming head-to-head."

Ahead of the Summer Olympics, Beijing had begun to step up its own health and safety standards across many elements of society and business, driven in part by a determination to clear the infamous smog that surrounded the city. The homegrown initiative, along with some well-publicized examples of lethal factory conditions around the region, accelerated a shift in mindset among global brands that outsourcing to developing markets did not absolve them of their responsibility to produce sustainably, and decision-making mattered across the global supply chain.

Sophia became even more passionate about bringing these two objectives—profitability and sustainability, then known as environmental and safety standards—out of their headlong collision course. By then, she had moved on to become the head of sustainability and emerging markets for a multinational manufacturer for the corporate real estate industry, which included producing furniture and décor for commercial spaces. In the process she became a pioneer of sustainable sourcing for wood, for example, or using materials free of formalde-hyde, and "all the things we take for granted now." But her early iterations of sustainable manufacturing came about through years of "blood, sweat, and tears, going from prototype to prototype."

At the same time, US and European brands were waking up to the fact that China was more than just the world's factory—it was a lucrative and booming consumer market in its own right. Increasingly, major corporations sought Sophia's expertise. Here was an opportunity to get it right on a global scale. During this process, Sophia realized she could connect these buyer desires for sustainable purchasing with the needed changes in the supply chain. So when the representatives from Fortune 500 companies flocked to the greater China region to expand their presence, she used the opportunity to guide them in their sustainable purchasing journey.

"I looked into their eyes to try to figure out what *they* cared about most: the air quality story, the water quality story? It was then I realized that those same purchasing executives needed to be led to make decisions in line with what their own CEOs and chief sustainability officers had taken a stand on, and which elements of sustainability mattered most to their local and regional clients and employees."

Sophia succeeded in raising awareness about the importance of topics such as indoor air quality and seeding a new level of consciousness among these company representatives about the pollution footprint these major brands were leaving on the other side of the world. Of course, this was well before there was a corporate language for carbon emissions or net-zero targets. It was the beginning of a long journey among consumer-facing global brands. But the passionate young advocate, who had previously established environmental programs in offices and schools in China on behalf of international NGOs, wanted to induce more change. She set her sights on influencing change from within, on the corporate side.

When she returned to the US, Sophia was determined to find a way to continue making a significant impact on sustainability. She set her sights on the transportation industry. In 2012 she began working with a major US airline, where she eventually became the airline's first chief sustainability officer, helping to shape the aviation industry by instigating real-time responses to climate crises. She led conversations about environment, social, and governance issues with investors, then *acted* on their concerns about brand reputation and financial value with practical, real-world solutions that would have far more long-term benefits than simple carbon taxes and offsets.

"The enemy is not flying. That would mean not going to your friend's wedding, taking a vacation, or taking a necessary business trip. The real enemy is unnecessary and 'unintentional' carbon, so let's pivot from capping flying to a conversation about what needs to change—the carbon intensity and what can actually be done within the operations and supply chain of flying that will reduce emissions." Sophia sought out partners who were willing and able to experiment in an industry steeped in safety concerns, and who could "show what was possible, one biofuel test, or electric ground service equipment charger at a time, without compromising safety."

But she was not content just achieving proof of concept within her organization. Sophia worked throughout the industry to show regulators and lawmakers what was achievable, "so we could say, 'Instead of seeing flying as a sin, give us tax breaks or support us through R&D, so that we can bring a solution to the industry, and scale.'"

Sophia got results. The airline implemented electric ground support vehicles such as baggage tractors and belt loaders at airports. It also made one of the earliest and largest hydrocarbon-based renewable jet fuel purchase agreements in aviation history by any airline in the world. Sophia also developed an onboard recycling system and even established a blue potato farm at one of the world's busiest airports as part of a larger effort to make airports more welcome places and engage crewmembers. By the time she left for Cognizant in 2020, Sophia had spearheaded multiple sustainability efforts. Under her leadership, the airline became the first to issue an ESG report aligned to the Sustainable Accounting Standards Board reporting standard, and the first to announce domestic carbon neutrality, earning her the US Environmental Agency's Climate Leadership Award in 2016. In 2020, the trailblazer was also named as one of the "top 30 people leading the climate charge" by *Bloomberg*.[1]

"I am genuinely proud of being on the vanguard of people who took what was a tree-hugging movement, put a suit on it, and walked it from the management level to the VP level, to the CEO's office, to the board," Sophia told me. "It's what I want to spend the rest of my life doing."

■ ■ ■

Sophia personifies the major shift from corporate social responsibility leaders to the role of chief sustainability officer whose strategy deeply connects into the heart of the overall business strategy. She brings the credentials, having worked around the globe in various capacities to understand how sustainability affects every function, from internal operations to the extended supply chain (multilevel systems thinking). She engages with stakeholders from the bottom up and builds relationships at the highest levels of leadership, earning trust and drawing in support from the CEO, board members, and the full length of the C-suite (stakeholder inclusion). She sets broad and ambitious goals not just for her department but also for the entire industry (long-term activation), and she's willing to take risks and experiment to demonstrate in concrete terms what can be done (disruptive innovation). In short, this archetypal CSO is propelled not just by the passion and idealism of SDG goals, but a solid track record of actions and real-world solutions.

All these ingredients are essential for becoming a great CSO, but I would add an overall ability to adapt, pivot, and even bound ahead of rapidly evolving conditions and metrics. Great CSOs tend to be comfortable with ambiguity and complexity, and it is just as well, because there is no playbook to fall back on. CSOs are not put off by not knowing all the answers; they are willing to work through the undefined spaces side by side with their stakeholders, wherever they sit in the organization. Above all, the CSO is collaborative. These executives may feel the need to be entrepreneurial to drive sustainability goals, but they understand they are fundamentally enablers, operating within the parameters of the business and finding where sustainability and business goals converge.

They also benefit from a degree of humility, encouraging those with a more intimate knowledge of their business unit or function to propose alternative solutions.

"My personal tool is coming to the table with as little ego as possible so that I can extract the best of people across functions," explained Sophia. "So if a shipping department comes up with something I haven't thought of because they are so close to the subject, I welcome their idea and steer the limelight in their direction, which helps me build on those relationships."

Similar to great sustainable CEOs, successful CSOs know how to embed a sense of purpose within a range of stakeholder groups. Some organizations are so large that they need centers of excellence to focus on the sustainability goal that makes the most sense for them. The transportation department could own climate and reducing emissions, for example, and a product division could own circularity. It works as long as it feeds back into a centralized goal in a controlled reporting environment that can show progress, or lack thereof. As Sophia put it, "The fundamental thing to do is take the CEO enterprise vision and the board's direction and translate that into your own specific ESG vision based on where your profitability comes from."

But CSOs cannot do it entirely on their own. They need sustainable leaders who can recognize and reward their efforts. As CEO, you need to clearly define the metrics and value creation of sustainable solutions so your sustainability leaders don't feel like they are tilting at windmills. Reward them for taking on the tough issues that may not yield results in the near term. Look for success beyond the usual key performance indicators (KPIs) and be prepared to invest more in the journey.

Front and Center

It helps that the role of sustainability leaders has evolved into something more central, rather than tangential, to the business. A few years ago, a sustainability role would not necessarily have been considered a fast track to a top leadership position. Sophia recalls needing a lot of patience and a thick skin. Sophia and her fellow CSOs had to take a more long-term view in the goals they set not just for the company but also for their own career paths.

"The original qualification was someone who was willing to take a hundred no's before they could even persuade a stakeholder to become a 'fence sitter.' The early generation of chief sustainability officers such as myself were willing to work on a five-year-plus time frame." Sophia contrasts this with the majority of management and executive track colleagues back then, who took a look at the sustainability space and rejected it.

"No sustainability for me; *I* want to be relevant," Sophia recalls many of them saying, by which of course they meant focusing on financial performance and having something to say on that quarterly call with shareholders (which, at that time, did not yet include sustainability efforts).

But, over the years, the Sophias of many major organizations have proven their business relevancy. Today's CSOs can come from varying backgrounds but, similar to sustainable CEOs, they tend to have experience across functions, and they most often possess knowledge of global supply chains, in addition to their experience in setting and driving sustainable development goals. Finance and corporate strategy are other common areas of cross-functional expertise. In an indication of how strategic the role has become to the operation of the business, the emphasis has shifted from experience in marketing, HR, and the legal department, where the focus may have been more on risk compliance and external messaging, to more strategic roles within the operations of the business.

The Archetypes

When we analyzed the backgrounds of CSOs in Fortune 250 companies to gain further insight into how some have approached the sustainability role, we learned that almost half were female, and 14% were the first to hold the role in their company. And the fact that the CSO role is a lot more diverse than other positions in the C-suite is promising. It may even indicate a way to improve diversity among future CEOs. Almost three out of four CSOs were promoted from within, having reached that level after holding different positions across the span of more than a decade.

Though no two CSOs are exactly alike, several archetypes have emerged that reflect the varying nature of the role and its objectives.

The Strategic Integrator

This individual has a track record of strategy or profit-and-loss ownership and is able to integrate sustainability priorities across product, operations, and brand. They tend to be a strategic visionary who can hit short-term priorities while keeping the long-term vision in focus. This leader also brings a holistic understanding of how sustainability efforts across organizations are mutually reinforcing. Typically, this CSO has transitioned from a strategic role or a leading position in an organization's business unit.

The Product Innovator

This CSO has experience successfully growing a sustainable product or service line in response to customer needs and sustainability priorities. Their strength is an ability to embed a sustainability lens to innovation processes. They are disruptive innovators who challenge traditional approaches to eliminate the "trade-off" between profitability and sustainability.

The Operations Guru

This leader has a track record of transforming operational practices in support of firm sustainability strategy. They are systems thinkers who thrive on solving complex problems. With a strong results orientation, these CSOs also enable leaders throughout the business to set and meet sustainability KPIs.

The Storyteller

Experienced in using data and emotion to tell a sustainability story, this CSO excels at connecting with stakeholders and building brand loyalty. They apply their deep understanding of customers and other stakeholders in decision-making while also connecting the tactical sustainability strategy to the broader corporate purpose and brand.

Maria Cristina Bifulco, CSO and group investor relations officer for Milan-based global cable manufacturer Prysmian, is from that storytelling stock. Prysmian, the world's largest producer of cables above and below ground for major infrastructure projects such as windfarms and fiber optic telecommunications, created the position for Cristina in early 2021, making her the first female direct report to long-time CEO Valerio Battista.

Now here's the thing about Prysmian, a 140-year-old company that was once the cable division of fabled tire manufacturer Pirelli: it comes across as a fusty, old-school engineering culture, and proud of it. Valerio is the first to admit that he can be a little gruff and tells me, in halting English, that he hates "talking the talk."

"I don't believe that proper management is to push for something that is just for show but is not supported by actions," he told me. "I want to be judged on how we act. What I don't like at all is people, colleagues, even members of the media who are talking without any substance."

Instead, the company leadership pride themselves on their pragmatism, with their sole focus on delivering results for their customers. It just so happens that Prysmian's $12 billion business is intrinsically sustainable because it provides interconnections between offshore windfarms and their rapidly growing markets. With an emphasis on sustainable innovation and lean manufacturing of its advanced cable systems, Prysmian, a UN Global Compact signatory, has been wired into the clean energy boom for decades. Even the vessel that lays high voltage lines onto the seabed is sustainable. Newly christened *Leonardo da Vinci*, the ship is designed for sustainable performance, with a green engine that has reduced emissions by 85% and low-consumption LED lighting.

Just don't ask Valerio to talk about it. That's for Cristina to communicate with Prysmian's internal and external stakeholders. She has been sharing that story through various global forums, skillful social media messaging, as well as through the group's magazine, *Insight*, with a depth of engagement that likely would not have been considered before her appointment. Valerio did launch a Sustainability Day in November 2020 as part of the company's annual stakeholder engagement, and almost half are ESG investors, yet he balked at the prospect of speaking at the event himself.

"If I can prove to him that it is something concrete, that is one thing," Cristina told me. "He cares about climate, and he cares about business. But if I ask him to do anything that's marketing or a conference, he threatens to fire me for wasting his time," the personable executive jokes, flashing a winning smile.

This CSO knows her team well as she gently coaxes them into greater self-awareness.

"When I start pushing sustainability and green initiatives internally my colleagues would stare at me because it is in our DNA, it's who we are! They don't understand why it's something we have to talk about, and in some sense, they take their sustainability for granted because our whole business is about clean energy and connectivity. When they design these cables they think about the protective casing, the local environment, the conditions on the ground, and they have been doing this since forever."

But it is motivating to tell that story internally and externally to the investor community.

"It makes my job easier that they know us well, they trust Valerio, they know we have a long-standing management that is hands-on, reliable, and accountable, and they appreciate the fact that we underpromise and overdeliver."

CEO Whisperer

One could argue that Cristina, similar to many successful CSOs, is as a kind of CEO whisperer. So is Anirban Ghosh, who performs the CSO role at Mahindra Group, the Indian conglomerate introduced in Chapter 4. Anirban, who believes that his role is to be an internal critic and advocate, is driving a broad decarbonization agenda for the $20 billion company, which describes itself as a "federation" of 150 companies in more than two dozen different sectors. He is widely credited as being the enabler for CEO Anand Mahindra's participation at the signing of the Paris Climate Accord in 2015—the sole representative of the corporate world. The Mahindra Group has since led the rest of the corporate world through its sustainability ambitions. In February 2019, Anand announced that his companies would together reach carbon neutrality by 2040.

There's plenty of careful coordination that happens before such a huge commitment can be made. Although these businesses are given the space to operate with relative independence, Mahindra's sustainability strategy, designed and led by Anirban, is centralized and includes a definition for practicing managers, with the flexibility for these diverse businesses to choose their areas of focus. Known as the "carbon choreographer" as he organizes the various energy-intensive businesses ranging from truck making to steelmaking, Anirban has been recognized by organizations such as the World Economic Forum for developing a sustainability dashboard, a rewards and recognition ecosystem for sustainability, and a metric that covers environmental impact and financial returns. Steered by this CSO, Mahindra became the first company in the world to commit to doubling its energy productivity, and the first Indian company to declare a carbon price within the business.

Key to accomplishing all this is an ability to speak the language of the business units—which Anirban's stint in marketing, sales, new business development, and strategy has equipped him to do—and make the alphabet soup of sustainability acronyms clear and accessible to all, including his boss.

"I decided to take the guy who used to run our tractor business in the US and put him in charge of sustainability. He is a very articulate guy who helps me with the acronyms I don't understand and has been an inexhaustible resource from the start. He became one of corporate India's most knowledgeable people in this subject at the time."

Not that the archetypal CSO seeks the recognition. In fact, as Sophia has experienced, a little internal ridicule can be a good thing if it signals that she is attempting something the naysayers contend is impossible.

Sophia says, "Never let perfection be the enemy of the good. Because I believe in sustainable aviation, I have seen many a satirical article written about me, and I am fine with it. I helped the system change for the outcome we needed, and that is progress."

Sustainable Leadership Takeaways

1. Be comfortable with ambiguity. Sustainability and its metrics are rapidly evolving. Not knowing all the answers, successful CSOs are willing to work through the undefined spaces side by side with other stakeholders, wherever they sit in the organization.

2. Be collaborative. Although it takes a degree of entrepreneurialism to push the SDG goals forward, as CSO you are fundamentally an enabler, operating within the parameters of the business and finding where the sustainability and business goals converge.

3. Share the limelight. Allow those with a more intimate knowledge of their business unit or function to propose a better solution. Welcome the ideas of other stakeholders and give them credit.

4. Work like a choreographer, smoothing the way for many moving parts. Some organizations are so large that they need centers of excellence to focus on an SDG goal that makes the most sense for them.

5. The ideal CSO takes steps to ensure that each sustainability project or initiative feeds back into a centralized goal in a controlled reporting environment that can show progress or lack thereof.

6. If you are a CEO or C-suite leader, recognize and reward the efforts of CSOs and other aspiring executives working on SDGs. Reward them for taking on the tough issues that may not yield results in the near term.

7. As CEO, clearly define the metrics and value creation of sustainable solutions, so your CSO and ESG leaders don't feel like they are tilting at windmills. Look for success beyond the usual KPIs and be prepared to invest more in the journey.

8

The Ecosystem

Individually we are one drop. Together we are an ocean.
—Ryunosoke Akutagawa, Japanese author

AURÉLIA NGUYEN HAD a mind-blowing to-do list.

As Managing Director of COVAX—a joint endeavor of the World Health Organization, UNICEF, the Coalition for Epidemic Preparedness Innovations, and GAVI, the Vaccine Alliance—it was her job to lead a global rollout of COVID-19 vaccines, ensuring vaccine equity for the most vulnerable populations of the world and saving millions of lives. She was charged with overseeing more than $10 billion in pledges to fund the procurement and ultimate delivery of billions of vaccine doses to 145 countries. To achieve this monumental task, Aurélia had to partner with and coordinate dozens of teams from business, nonprofit and government sectors, leveraging their diverse expertise while rallying them around a singular, urgent purpose at lightning speed.

A little less than two years into the pandemic, I sat down with Aurélia to interview her for Russell Reynold's "Redefiners" podcast where we explore how daring leaders from across industries and around

119

the globe are redefining their organizations—and themselves—to create extraordinary impact in today's rapidly changing world. I was intrigued to learn how this former GlaxoSmithKline director managed to maintain her cool under fire, with so many governments, NGOs and bureaucrats circling around her as she attempted to encourage, persuade, and cajole business leaders and wealthier nations to do the right thing on vaccine equity.

As CEO of a global company, I was all too aware of the pressure of leading through a pandemic. We all felt it as we safeguarded our health, protected our families, and maintained our professional lives, all the while making sure our employees were safe and their jobs were secure despite so many uncertainties in the business and economic climate. At RRA, we also like to think we did our part to help mitigate the impact of the pandemic by participating in the WHO Foundation's borderless fundraising campaign Go Give One, where a $5 donation provided a vaccine to someone in a country who could not afford it. But I could only compare what Aurélia accomplished to the Berlin Airlift in 1948, when the U.S. began a massive delivery of food, medicine, and water to the citizens of West Berlin, whose access to the world had been choked off by the Soviet Union's blockade. Yet COVAX was dealing with thousands more communities, billions of individuals and essentially half the world's population. Realizing the scale and stakes of her achievement was humbling indeed.

"Did you ever feel overwhelmed?" I asked her.

"It was a daunting prospect, and it's true there were moments I felt a bit out of my depth," Aurélia shared. As mother to two young boys who needed a lot of "hands-on care," she took a beat to discuss this move with her family before "jumping in with both feet" because she knew she would need to somehow find that work/life balance. But despite the challenge of balancing her personal and professional obligations Aurélia, who is French-Vietnamese, felt the "pressing call" to get involved.

"It's a time when many people in their respective roles have really felt the need to step up. It is almost like a war effort. It demands a lot of personal sacrifice for a wider goal."

The sheer enormity of the endeavor also required her to "get comfortable" with not having all the answers. She realized that "it is not all on one person. One does it with one's leadership, one's board, and pulling together incredible teams."

In other words, this sustainable leader saw herself as a kind of collaborator-in-chief. She wasn't alone. Rather, her challenge was how to get the best out of each actor and leverage their various strengths around the mission. Making things happen at this level requires an entire ecosystem of resources and knowledge. And it takes a special kind of sustainable leader—one with the relationship network, diplomatic skills, logistical chops, big picture vision, and humility—to know where, when, and how to ask for help.

"We're not starting from scratch. We're working with organizations that have long been in existence. Yet you don't have command and control over them. It's all in how you harness their capabilities around answering this crisis under unforeseen pressure. Being able to build consensus around what each organization brings, whether that's funding, technical expertise, the ability to advocate, then harnessing that energy toward specific milestones and deliverables is, I think, the critical path to take."

■ ■ ■

Whether it's dealing with the social, health, and economic issues of vaccine inequity on a global scale, or dramatically accelerating the pace of their climate goals, sustainable leaders understand the necessity of including a wide swath of external stakeholders across multiple industries and sectors. And, post-pandemic, seeing the way this vaccine effort moved mountains, the business world now has a crisper view of how we can hit sustainability goals like inclusivity, cleaner water, poverty alleviation, and other health issues on a massive scale.

The process is highly complex, with many moving parts (multi-systems thinking). It can be rife with frustrations and roadblocks, which I will touch upon later in this chapter. But the good news is that, as COVAX and many other organizations have proven, there are ways to create ecosystems to navigate these challenges, and it's well worth the endeavor at a moment in history when having meaningful impact requires the participation of all kinds of organizations. In fact, for the size and scope of the transformation that is needed, I'm not sure that we have a choice, as the existential challenges we face are more than one sector can handle.

We also need to step back and take a larger view of the world and raise the bar for what we can accomplish way beyond our own operational footprint.

At RRA, we analyzed opportunities for effective corporate/social sector partnerships, and three key lessons emerged:

- The need for corporations to make meaningful commitments to collaborate with nonprofits, recognizing the mutual benefits of partnership and fostering trust.
- The need for clarity and specificity. A clear value proposition underpins successful collaborations and ensures that decision making stays focused on maximum mutual impact, rather than individual organizational needs.
- A focus on strengths. Develop a capabilities orientation that recognizes the comparative advantages of each side within a network to maximize partnership impact. And focus on your own core capabilities as you build out that broader social goal.

In other words, do the research to discover what already exists, then leverage what's out there. Often there are building blocks for meeting ambitious sustainability goals already in place. For example, in the unprecedented mobilization of what was close to a billion doses of vaccine at the time of writing, COVAX was co-led by GAVI, which was an alliance in and of itself. The organization had, for the previous two decades, already been working with members of the public health community and had a vast network of funders, public officials, and politicians in developing countries, civil society organizations, and technical partners.

Of course, there was plenty of innovation, too. The COVID vaccine rollout was a combination of solutions on the fly, particularly when it came to liaising with Big Pharma companies to procure large-scale quantities of something still under development, then tapping the existing infrastructure for the massive rollout of doses with limited shelf lives to markets with often complex and limited storage requirements. Scaling up the delivery also required creativity, coming up with mechanisms to indemnify the businesses, protecting them against potential liability, or working with external partners to develop blockchain technology to ensure data integrity for vaccine recipients. When I spoke with Aurélia, she was also considering partnering with a company that could help COVAX use satellite imagery to find communities so remote that they weren't visible on official mapping systems.

Enabler-in-Chief

The beauty of the right partnership is in the possibility of scaling something for the social and environmental good many times more than your own corporation's footprint, with external expertise that can slice through to a solution faster and with more focus. The core philosophy of a company such as Salesforce lends itself to the creation of an ecosystem for the advancement of a sustainability goal. The San Francisco–headquartered software company is a global leader in customer relationship management. Its founder and co-CEO Marc Benioff has transformed the business software industry, enabling and empowering other organizations through the cutting-edge technology his company provides.

Marc, who is known for his philanthropy and activist causes, has applied his leadership, networking/collaboration, and technological skills to one of his greatest personal passions: the ocean. In 2015, after reading an article in the *New York Times* that warned we are facing rapid increases in the loss of marine wildlife, he felt compelled to seek out expertise that was beyond the scope of Salesforce. The article referenced the research of University of California, Santa Barbara professor Doug McCauley, so Marc emailed him and invited him to lunch. The two men talked for hours about ocean science, brainstorming about how they could leverage the power of research to prevent, and possibly reverse, the crisis. Eventually, Marc appointed Doug leader of the Benioff Ocean Initiative, which links government, scientists and researchers, NGOs, community leaders, grassroots activists, and other changemakers around the world to execute science-based solutions.

The initiative created an AI-powered whale detection system that helps ships slow down to avoid running into the mammals (which I certainly could have used on my past transatlantic crossings). Similar technological solutions have been used to build shark detection systems, protect marine ecosystems, and combat plastic pollution. But Marc did not stop there. A conversation with Dr. Jane Goodall, the famed English primatologist and anthropologist, got him thinking about the forests. "She asked me what I was doing about our forests and trees, and I didn't know what to say. While I thought about our oceans quite a bit, I had not thought about trees, which are nature's purifiers and the single most effective device we have to pull carbon out of the atmosphere."

Marc has gone on to work with Dr. Goodall, as well as other scientists and business leaders, to launch 1t.org—a global movement to conserve, restore, and grow 1 trillion trees through multi-stakeholder partnerships. Fifty corporations and governments across the world, including in the US, European Union, Canada, the United Kingdom, China, India, Pakistan, and Columbia, have pledged to plant billions of trees by 2030 with the ultimate goal of sequestering 100 gigatons of carbon. It's already yielded impressive results. Two years in and 1t.org has already reached the goal to conserve, restore, and grow over 3.6 billion trees, including 43 million from Salesforce. Salesforce is also building an ecosystem around "ecopreneurship" in partnership with the World Economic Forum through UpLink, a platform Salesforce developed that has so far connected 30,000 innovators dedicated to developing climate solutions around the world.

"We all have to do something, but we cannot all do everything. If we think we are going to do everything, we're going to get lost," Marc told me. "Reaching the Paris Agreement goals will require transformation on a global scale. We all have a role to play. Together, we can unlock the ability of every company, individual, and nation state to take action on climate change and save our planet."

Public/Private

Walter Schalka, CEO of Brazilian pulp and paper giant Suzano SA, the world's largest exporter of eucalyptus, is justifiably proud of the fact that his company plants 800,000 trees a day. Yet he insists that corporations cannot do it alone. They need government action. In 2020, he signed a letter together with other CEOs to the Brazilian government's Amazon Council, led by vice president Hamilton Mourão, to demand comprehensive action to fight illegal deforestation. He has been seeking a regulated carbon market to help finance forest regeneration.

As a leading member of the Brazilian Coalition on Climate, Forests and Agriculture—a public/private group of industry, academic, and government leaders—he told me, "Intra-industry collaboration, including with our competitors, is key. We are not losing our competitive edge. Because if we don't work together, despite being in another company, industry, or country, we can't make progress."

Of course, your own ecosystem does not have to span the globe. Powerful movements can also start small, even in a remote village.

The Miracle Bean

On the outskirts of Bikaner, a small town in the northern Indian province of Rajasthan, near the border of Pakistan, more than 1,500 lives are changing. Thanks to an initiative led by Belgian-based chemicals company Solvay in partnership with cosmetics giant L'Oréal, consumer goods and chemicals company Henkel, HiChem Paint Technologies, and the Indian NGO TechnoServe, an entire community of women are becoming "agri-preneurs" by cultivating guar, a hardy legume that grows well in those desert conditions. This diverse, drought-resistant bean has thickening, emulsifying gelling and binding properties that make it one of the most essential agrochemical ingredients on the planet, with safe and environmentally friendly uses in the food, textile, cosmetics, oil, and pharmaceutical industries, to name a few.

About 80% of the world's supply of guar beans is grown in India, and 70% is farmed in Rajasthan. But, for Ilham Kadri, CEO of Solvay, whom you met in Chapter 3, launching the Sustainable Guar Initiative

(SGI) in 2015 was not just about improving and stabilizing guar yields for profit. The idea was to create an ecosystem for guar cultivation that would make production more sustainable through the use of climate-smart agricultural practices and improve the region's climate preparedness and the region's resilience. The program would also enhance the livelihood of guar bean farmers by ensuring their income durability, protecting local resources, and enhancing sustainable practices for rain-fed guar production. They would also be taught cutting-edge agronomy along with tree plantation for biodiversity benefits such as improved soil structure.

Beyond these benefits, the partnership focused on the social impact its efforts in the region could have, particularly as it related to empowering female farmers. The women of Bikaner hold a decision-making role in farming families in terms of meal preparation in their homes and in guar cultivation, so participants of the SGI focused on improving their knowledge and skills, training them not just in best practices for guar farming but also teaching and enabling them to plant fruit trees and vegetables in their own backyards. About 1,000 kitchen gardens were established through the effort with an average annual yield of almost 300 pounds each. Not only could the female farmers feed their families with their small crops but also they could sell the excess fruits and vegetables in the local markets to earn income in addition to their guar cultivation.

The women of Bikaner were made aware of the benefits of different kinds of vegetables and given recipes and food preparation tips. They were given reference material about what time of year to sow the seeds for different plants, and how to maintain their gardens. Among the many things these women were taught was that spinach and fenugreek grow well in sandy soil. These leafy greens, which greatly enhanced nutrition for themselves and their families, hadn't previously been available in the region's markets, and they now they are a staple part of their diet.

Puzzle Pieces

But, as Ilham discovered, there was more that needed to be done to fully give these Indian matriarchs agency to build their incomes and feed their families. On an in-person tour of the local farming community, Ilham met a middle-aged woman in a bright orange sari proudly showing off all the food and guar she had grown. The top executive stopped to introduce herself and then asked her a few questions. "What has this initiative done for you?" she asked.

"Before I was like this," the woman, whom we will call Anita, replied, holding a fold of her sari over her face to indicate that she felt invisible. Then she dropped the fabric and beamed, "Now I am like this!"

What made the biggest impact in this woman's life was something that most in the developed world take for granted. Prior to the SGI, this female farmer felt she could not prepare food while she was menstruating. She felt unclean.

"A large [percentage] of women in India do not have access to sanitary products, and use alternatives, such as rags, ash, sand, and husks," explained Rajnesh Sentu, SGI project leader at Techno-Serve India.

So another part of the SGI mission involved teaching these women and adolescent girls about basic biology. TechnoServe stepped in to help women adopt hygiene practices that would enhance their well-being and normalize, or destigmatize, perceptions about menstruation. Henkel volunteer employees, meanwhile, donated sanitary napkins, and women were set up in business to sell these items to others in their community.

"Now I am like you and can cook for my children," Anita proudly told Ilham. "I am not impure like I used to think. I know that hygiene and cleaning keep us safe. . . . I can collect clean water from the few times it rains here, and I can grow vegetables in my garden. I take pride in it and the kitchen feeds my family with high-nutrition vegetables I had never cooked before. My kids and also my girls can go to school and they can learn. I am independent, a happier mother and a proud woman."

Still, not all the pieces of the puzzle were in place. Now that Anita had her own income, she needed to put it somewhere, "but I am not bankable," she said. The local banks wouldn't accept her business unless she was accompanied by a man. So Ilham reached out to financial technology experts to explore how blockchain—a security form of digital identity management—could give women like Anita access to financial services.

What brought this wide array of corporate partners together on the SGI was a desire to increase yields sustainably, providing a vital ingredient for a vast consumer goods supply chain—everything from shampoo to cat food to gluten-free cupcakes. But the more Ilham delved into the conditions on the ground in Bikaner, the more she understood what needed to be done to fully engage these female farmers, who were key players in the supply chain for multiple industries. The issues were wide-ranging, but Solvay's ecosystem was able to pull in local, regional, and global stakeholders with diverse strengths to overcome each obstacle as it arose.

"If you want to achieve something at scale, you need partnerships," explained Ilham, who invited her customer P&G to join the initiative, alongside Henkel and L'Oréal, knowing that they would welcome the opportunity to add a "sustainably sourced" label on their products and "live their own sustainability values and built market share amongst environmentally conscious consumers."

But perhaps the most excited participant in the project was Ilham herself. Bikaner, and the women she met there, made a lasting impression on her. It was the first time the chief executive fully appreciated the link between improving the conditions of individuals that far down in the supply chain and profit. These Rajasthani farmers were more engaged and productive as a direct result of the ecosystem that supplied them with the tools for financial independence, physical well-being, dignity, and respect.

"Meeting those women had a profound impact on me and they will forever be a part of my journey," Ilham told me, proudly pointing to a framed picture of Anita above her desk. "I always had a sense of how much sustainability matters for its own sake. But now I understand it is also a value proposition. It's good for business, the community, and beyond."

From Critics to Collaborators

Whether its guar yields, vaccine rollouts, or shared passions such as saving trees and oceans, sustainable leaders need to be able to rally their external partners around that common cause, whatever their vested interests may be. But successful ecosystems aren't always the result of alignment among stakeholders. People and organizations on seemingly opposite sides of an issue can form powerful partnerships when a common objective comes into focus, as was the case when Duke Energy CEO Lynn Good, whom you met in Chapter 1, took the time to truly listen to the concerned citizens of Asheville, North Carolina.

"Climate is on everybody's mind and it's a conversation we're having everywhere," Lynn told me. "We have to be engaged at the local, state, and national level with all parties, whether they are environmental activists, manufacturers, low-income families. . . ."

In May 2015, when Duke Energy announced the planned closure of Asheville's coal-fired power plant and its replacement with a large natural gas power plant and 45 miles of new high-voltage lines, there was an outcry. Residents across the region submitted more than 10,000 comments online in opposition to their initial plan and pushed for an alternative based on greener energy sources. Duke Energy heard them and retracted the proposal in favor of codeveloping a new solution in collaboration with various community stakeholders. That's when the Blue Horizons Project was born.

Duke Energy teamed up with the City of Asheville and Buncombe County, as well as local businesses, institutions, and environmental advocates. The aim was to enlist public support and provide easy access to resources that would enable everyone to be a part of creating a clean energy future.

"Robust stakeholder engagement has been incredibly important," Lynn told me. "The people of Asheville have chosen to live in the mountains. It's a university town, and they are an environmentally sensitive community."

One of the main goals of the coalition was to reduce energy use by creating a demand-response system, allowing Duke Energy to control the thermostats of its home and business customers for maximum efficiency. Duke Energy and its local partners also worked with low-income and diverse communities in the area to provide free energy efficiency and weatherization services, as well as home heating assistance programs. Other Blue Horizon goals that were achieved include the following:

- Retiring Asheville's coal-fired power plant
- Building a smaller, two-unit, natural gas plant

- Developing at least 15 MW of solar generation and at least five MW of battery storage
- Delaying the construction of a combustion turbine "peaker" plant beyond 2023; the community wanted to use existing resources rather than add another generator to the region, and a peaker, which operates only at times of maximum use, would by definition be less energy efficient and unsuitable for alternative fuel use

---

Fruits of Engagement

- 2,567 residential customers enrolled in Duke Energy's EnergyWise program.
- 895 commercial and industrial customers enrolled in the EnergyWise Business program.
- 150 free weatherization upgrades and nine whole-home retrofits for low-income households.
- 700 homes and 92 businesses reduced energy consumption.

The success of these multi-stakeholder engagements has inspired Lynn to start thinking about other innovative ways to generate energy that are compatible with local conditions and expectations. One possibility is using the fallow land of the old tobacco farms of northeastern Carolina for large-scale solar farms. Old tobacco farming families that have been struggling can turn their disused acres into sources of income and provide customers in other parts of the service territory with the clean energy they love. As Lynn explained, "We need to work together to help shape what's achievable, so that we have broad support for the pace of change, and so that we are listening to how communities want to be a part of that change."

Connecting these different groups requires a shared vision based on clarity and commonality. Everyone needs to understand how the goal benefits all parties. The collaboration also needs to be diverse. You cannot leave anyone out of the conversation, least of all grassroots organizations. The Blue Horizon Project expanded to include more partners in the conversation as it recognized the evolving needs of Asheville's citizens, including nonprofit research institutes to provide credible, third-party verified data. Recognizing that communication was key, it also hired marketing groups to make sure the information was clear and accessible to everyone concerned.

The fact that Duke Energy was able to embrace a holistic approach, creating solutions geared toward the needs and wants all members of the community, helped the company profit from efficiencies it might not have otherwise sought in the area. Most utility companies would have focused on solving problems through technology, increasing their generation, transmission, or distribution infrastructure. But, by embracing input from all parties through the Blue Horizon ecosystem, Duke Energy did much more, gaining deeper insights into grid benefits for battery storage, data-driven energy management, and other technically sound solutions aligned with local interests. Above all, the utility giant had gained the trust of stakeholders who had previously been among their harshest critics.

Common Denominators

Again, these broad collaborations are not easy. It requires limitless patience, the humility to listen, and the compassion to see the issue from the other stakeholders' point of view. Kate Brandt, Google's chief sustainability officer, whom you met in Chapter 3, has gone through the process of partnering across sectors on multiple occasions throughout her career in government and at the corporate level. When it comes to working with other corporate players on ways to reach zero emissions, Kate noted global public-private partnership examples such as the Clean Energy Buyers Association and Sustainable Energy for All, though "candidly I am struggling with that right now. There is definitely a need and opportunity to do more together."

Industry collaborations are particularly challenging because "you have to figure out how this is a win for everyone. How do you keep it noncompetitive? How do you keep it focused on the systems change?"

Often, she finds, the different stakeholders will meet, say the right things, and little if anything will come of it.

"No one wants to share what they are thinking, instead just waiting to hear what everyone else says," she told me. "And then you get the common denominator problem. Whatever statement or proclamation you are making is driven by the company that's the least ambitious."

Public-Private partnerships are hard but "so, so necessary." The sheer cost and complexity of ambitious SDGs such as zero emissions, developing solutions such as sustainable aviation fuel and low carbon concrete, for example, requires collective action from the private sector across industries.

One solution Kate found was to leverage the public sector as a test bed for programs and a convenor of corporate participation. That's what happened in the US Department of Defense when the Navy, during the Obama Administration, committed to running its ships and planes on advanced biofuels. As a huge engine of procurement, that decision sent a demand signal to the private sector. The bold goal setting drove certainty, inspiring companies such as Boeing and Maersk to step up.

"They figure, if that is where the military is going, I'd better pay attention."

Can-Do Climate

There can also be moments when a powerful ecosystem evolves organically, with seemingly little effort, almost as if it were meant to be.

In November 2021, I traveled to Scandinavia to meet with a cluster of sustainable leaders whose bold goal settings and achievements had impressed me so much I wasn't content just to meet with them on a Zoom call. It was during that brief window before the Omicron variant hit, when international travel was less restricted, and I just had to take this opportunity to talk with these CEOs face-to-face in the same time zone.

My first meeting was in Copenhagen with Søren Skou, CEO of AP Moller-Maersk, which had recently announced plans to launch its first carbon-neutral fleet by 2023, fast-tracked seven years ahead of its original deadline of 2030 because of "advances in technology and increasing customer demand for sustainable supply chains," according to a company statement. The shipping industry, which transports about 80% of global trade, is responsible for 3% of global carbon emissions, and Maersk controls the largest container line in the world. The energy used by most of these ships, called *bunker fuel*, is cheap and nasty stuff, prompting international regulators to require a dramatic reduction of sulfur content in marine fuels, as well as reduction of nitrogen oxide emissions.

Søren had gone all-in, with more than $1 billion invested in creating a decarbonized fleet. Because ships have a life expectancy of 20 to 25 years,[1] meeting the industry goal of carbon neutral by 2050 requires aggressive action and intensive investment as its current fleet would need to be replaced by 2030. Yet it was by no means clear at that point where or how an adequate supply of green energy—methanol, ethanol, and green ammonia—could be sourced.

"Our ambition to have a carbon-neutral fleet by 2050 was a moonshot when we announced it in 2018," Søren said. "Today we see it as a challenging, yet achievable target to reach."

As we spoke in Søren's office on the Esplanaden overlooking the pristine waters of Copenhagen's inner harbor, he was candid about the unprecedented challenges Maersk was facing. It was the classic chicken-and-egg problem. No one was making green fuel because no one was buying it, so the green ships came first. (To that end, Maersk became a founding member of the First Movers Coalition, a new platform for companies to make purchasing commitments that create new market demand for low-carbon technologies.)

Then along came fellow Dane, Mads Nipper, CEO of Ørsted, the world's largest developer of offshore wind power, whom you met in Chapter 3. Ørsted, among the first to prove that green energy could be produced at scale, teamed up with Maersk, Copenhagen Airports, heavy-duty truck maker DSV Panalpina, shipping and logistics company DFDS, and SAS Airlines to develop a hydrogen and e-fuel production facility by 2025. When fully operational, this facility will deliver more than 250,000 tons of sustainable fuels for busses, trucks, airplanes, and, of course, ships. With a potential capacity of 1.2 GW, it would be one of the largest facilities of its kind in the world, which, when fully operational, could reduce annual carbon emissions by 850,000 tons. It will take time to ramp up production of these renewables, which are many times more expensive than traditional fuels. But the hope is that this platform will inspire similar demand and supply-side, cross-industry partnerships to scale up the supply side of sustainable fuels.

"Many of these things are not hard to do, but they are hard to do at scale, and for that you need partnerships," explained Mads. "You've got to collaborate across industries and within your industry to create demand and make things move faster."

Then along came Yara, a Norway-based global conglomerate first introduced in Chapter 4, that, among many other things, is a manufacturer of nitrogen fertilizer. In March 2021, Yara and Maersk teamed up with the Port of Singapore, the shipyard Keppel Offshore, ship manager Fleet Management, and Sumitomo, the Japanese conglomerate to be among the first to set up a comprehensive and competitive supply chain for the provision of green ammonia. They began with a feasibility study for ammonia bunkering at the world's busiest bunkering port—Singapore. A dual-fuel ammonia engine was already under development by Maersk, but they still had supply, safety, and infrastructure challenges to resolve. Each partner is applying their expertise: Maersk and Fleet Management are developing safe and reliable bunkering procedures, Sumitomo is focused on supply chain issues such as transportation and storage, Keppel will design the ammonia bunkering vessels, and Yara is in charge of a feasibility analysis for supplying the ammonia.[2]

"What we must do is bigger than any one industry, any one company," Yara CEO Svein Tore Holsether told me.

■ ■ ■

So, in effect, all three of the CEOs I met with were already in the process of solving each other's problems. I came away from my conversations with a sense of perfect circularity. Perhaps it is part the culture of the region, where the paramount importance of sustainability is in the air you breathe. Maybe this can-do climate is because the business community is comparatively small and tightknit. Whatever the reasons, I came across many Scandinavian leaders who had made historically significant strides toward not just their own sustainability goals but also those of much broader communities. There's a boldness, which I will explore in Chapter 9, which may stem in part from the fact that these leaders understand they are not in this alone. They have an acute awareness of each other, what they are doing, and how that fits into the larger sustainability story. Many of them were already friends or, at a minimum, friendly acquaintances with a deep mutual respect. Either way, they are cultivating an openness, setting aside competitiveness within their own industries to move mountains.

Over an office lunch of some of the freshest sushi I have ever tasted, Yara's Svein shared how as "an introverted Norwegian," building those alliances took effort. And yet he has faced criticism for engaging too much externally. Unfazed, he appointed a deputy CEO to help him balance internal responsibilities.

"We don't need miracles to get this done," Svein told me. "We need trust across the value chain, and the political will, which is why I will continue to be out there. We need each other; we don't have a choice."

Sustainable Leadership Takeaways

1. Get comfortable with not having all the answers. Leverage the diverse expertise of your partners as you rally them around a singular, urgent purpose.

2. When working within these broad alliances, you are not in command and control. Rather, you are a kind of collaborator-in-chief, getting the best out of each participant and maximizing their strengths.

3. Creating an ecosystem takes relationship networking, diplomatic skills, logistical chops, big-picture vision, and humility—to know where, when, and how to ask for help.

4. Get government involved. These movements require political will, and industry leaders pay attention to the direction of economic engines such as the military.

5. Build consensus on what each organization brings, whether that's funding, technical expertise, or the ability to advocate. Then harness that energy toward specific milestones and deliverables.

(continued)

6. Be specific. A clear value proposition underpins successful collaborations and ensures that decision-making stays focused on maximum mutual impact rather than individual organizational needs.

7. Even your harshest critics can become allies when you focus on common interests as opposed to stakeholder positions. Engage and listen. Courage, commitment, and patience are essential tools to overcome differences.

8. Engage third-party support. External organizations such as nonprofits or academic institutions can provide expertise that brings a sense of credibility, smoothing the way for a project by overcoming community distrust or resentment.

9

The Money That Follows

We measure everything—why not governance?
      —Mohammed "Mo" Ibrahim, Sudanese-British technology mogul

ONE BY ONE, they pulled out of the Russian market, with billions of dollars in assets and revenue on the line. As they watched in horror like the rest of us Vladimir Putin's February 24, 2022, invasion of Ukraine—seeing in real time the footage of a military force gone medieval on civilians—the CEOs and executive boards of many of the biggest corporations in the world divested with lightning speed.[1] In fact, their reaction times were arguably faster, in some cases pulling the trigger before sanctions were announced by the US government and its NATO allies.

At the time of writing, more than 300 multinationals, from consumer goods companies to tech giants such as Meta, have announced plans to unwind their investments in Russia, however complicated the process of extricating themselves from relationships that span decades. Some of the most dramatic drawdowns were from oil companies:

- Shell, which announced its intention to withdraw from its involvement in all Russian hydrocarbons, including crude oil, petroleum products, gas and liquefied natural gas, in phases, though it would immediately stop all spot purchases of Russian crude oil; it will also shut its service stations, aviation fuels, and lubricants operations in Russia

- bp, which said it would exit its almost 20% stake in Rosneft, the Russian state-controlled oil company, as well as its joint ventures in Russia
- ExxonMobil, which vowed to discontinue operations of the Sakhalin 1 project, one of the world's top-10 record-setting oil fields it runs on behalf an international consortium of Japanese, Indian, and Russian companies

Everyone, no matter the industry, was forced to reexamine their ties to Russia, including Apple, Dell, Disney, PepsiCo, Visa, American Express, Ford, Unilever, McDonald's, and so on. No matter how deep and long-standing their relationships with Russian business partners and consumers, they embarked on the costly and complex process of extricating themselves, fully aware that any association with a pariah state became toxic for everyone, from consumers to shareholders. Early in the conflict, for example, dock workers in England even refused to unload barrels of Russian crude. The world had spoken and, seemingly overnight, solidarity with and support of the Ukrainian people became an SDG. Or I should say, the SDG for this moment in history. The global reaction against Russia's leadership may reshape the world's economy for decades to come.

One could argue the merits or effectiveness of some of these sanctions, which negatively affect average Russian citizens who had no role to play in the invasion and may well have been against it. I am no foreign policy expert, and, as I watched all this play out in real time, could not say for certain if these corporate exits would somehow curb the Russian leader's territorial ambitions.

But that does not render the bold actions made by these corporations any less significant. The resounding message they sent was that we cannot, under any circumstances, continue to do business with bad actors, and billions in losses are nothing compared with the unprovoked atrocities and war crimes being committed by a military aggressor.

Shell learned this lesson quickly when it had to answer for a heavily discounted consignment of 100 metric tons of Russian crude it had purchased in advance of the Ukraine conflict. In response to a wave of censure over the deal, including from the Ukraine's foreign minister, the company's leadership apologized: "We are acutely aware that our decision last week to purchase a cargo of Russian crude oil to be refined into products like petrol and diesel . . . was not the right one and we are sorry," said Shell CEO Ben van Beurden, who promised to contribute profits from their remaining supplies of Russian oil to a fund dedicated to humanitarian aid for the Ukraine.[2]

Even Japanese fast fashion company Uniqlo came under similar approbation when it initially dug in its heels about staying in the Russian market, then swiftly changed tact and suspended its operations there. Meanwhile, other companies have set examples, with Goldman Sachs as the first big US bank to exit, followed within hours of its announcement by JPMorgan Chase, and every other US global bank and financial services company.

And yet the motivations behind these corporate actions were not just to avoid scandal or do no harm. Every day there were reports of a major corporation doing something out of humanitarian impulse, such as Ikea and the Ingka Foundation, which committed $11 million for aid groups to ship essential products into Ukraine, or H&M, which donated clothes and other necessities, along with L'Oréal, which donated more than $250,000 worth of hygiene products. Airbnb and multiple European hotel chains provided free lodging to Ukraine refugees. Drugmakers Eli Lilly and Merck offered COVID-19 treatments, insulin, and money for life-saving medical devices. Not least, right at the start of the conflict, Elon Musk's SpaceX donated Starlink satellite internet terminals so that the besieged nation would not be cut off from the world, or each other, and more than a dozen European telecom providers scrapped roaming charges and offered free international calls to the people of Ukraine. In effect, corporations stepped in to offer funds, services, and essential items where government and nonprofits did not have the logistical infrastructure or resources to move as swiftly.

I am old enough to remember the 1980s, when the pace for imposing sanctions on South Africa's Apartheid regime was glacial.

Even though it was a much smaller market for most Western businesses and brands, with financial exposure a fraction of what companies faced for writing off Russian business, it took the span of a decade for the corporate world and governments to respond to the evils of Johannesburg's racist oppression. Apartheid didn't play out with 24/7 live streaming, nor was it in the form of sudden and shocking military action—a brutal ground war beamed into our living rooms through wall-to-wall news coverage. And it did not happen in 2022. We are living in a time when the consciousness of corporate leadership has been raised to a whole new level.

Since 2020, the beginning of the Decade of Action and, of course, the global pandemic, awareness at the top has accelerated at an unprecedented pace. I may be proven wrong by the time this book is released, but I predict that this quick corporate reaction to Russia's aggression may ultimately help to set up faster reduction of fossil fuels. It is a different world, where shareholders, C-suite executives, board members, and every stakeholder who influences how money is invested, who gets hired, and how leaders are compensated understand what it means to serve the greater good.

■ ■ ■

Had it not been for all the work that has been done by sustainable leaders as they telegraph and act on their SDGs internally and across their industries, I am not so sure we would have seen corporations react so rapidly and uniformly, out of a sense of urgent, moral responsibility. What we were witnessing has been a quantum leap in how businesses view their role on the world stage and a positive result of this decade's seemingly endless onslaught of social inequity, climate disaster, and human tragedy. Doing the right thing is now inextricably linked with corporate governance; it is paramount, sitting at the top of the board's agenda and not just one of many strategic goals.

Are we there yet? Not quite. And decision-making in other sustainability matters will likely not happen at the same rapid-fire pace of the Ukraine crisis, which was a unique moment in history. But one big takeaway from this tragic period in our history is that meaningful action can happen with striking velocity when there is real alignment between board members and the CEO. With the right board composition, major investment decisions are no longer akin to turning around a massive cruise ship. They can be powered through when the stakes are clear and foot dragging risks damage to the brand that can do far more long-term damage to profits than the near-term financial exposure.

Jim Hagemann Snabe, chair of Siemens and Maersk, likens this need to move forward and focus on the future to a board lunch.

"I have an interesting rule of thumb, which is, we'll discuss the past until lunch, and we'll discuss the future after lunch," he told me. "At the beginning of my chairmanships, lunch started a little bit late because the tradition was to dwell on the past. But nowadays we have early lunches because it's obvious that in these times of such dramatic change we need to have a discussion about what our assumptions are for the future."

That future includes a greater willingness to take risks.

"Many boards use a lot of time to make sure that you have good governance and you are compliant, manage risk, but that's not about avoiding risk," Jim observed. "I actually believe that in times of radical change, not taking a risk is the biggest risk you can take."

Jim proudly pointed to the example of Maersk where senior leadership overcame inhibitions about costs and gains with the audacious decision-making we discussed in previous chapters. Although the mindset of many board members is to plan the future in a linear fashion, "we need exponential. We need dramatic acceleration. And so to do that you need to have courage."

It also requires challenging assumptions.

"One assumption that I think is wrong when it comes to sustainability is that it is a cost. It is going to be taking money away from shareholders to use it on the planet. I just don't think that holds true anymore."[3] Too much has already changed for that cost- and risk-averse mindset to be viable. As the revolution continues, its full effects are still not yet fully known. We are in a perfect storm of digital disruption, pandemic, racial and social crises, imminent climate disaster and a massive rethink of our workplace culture (the Great Resignation), and, most recently, a brutal ground war visible in real time, has resulted in this seismic shift in the attitudes and actions of businesses' top leadership.

Consider the fact that 74% of nomination and governance committee (NomCo) chairs from leading companies around the world provide sustainability oversight, according to our research.[4] Sustainability is increasingly seen as a critical leadership competency, with NomCo chairs saying it was important or extremely important in the selection of board directors (63%) and senior executives (77%). Both these numbers were on the rise: 52% of respondents said this was more important now than in past years for board directors, and 58% said the same about senior executives.

NomCo chairs play a powerful role on boards, influencing everything from who becomes CEO to who joins the board and which board directors hold leadership positions. Sustainability was top of mind for these board leaders, signaling once again that what is happening is not greenwashing but a growing awareness that companies don't need to sacrifice profits to take action that improves the world—and in fact doing good helps companies do well.

The evidence is in that the pressure for corporations to perform better on issues such as diversity and climate is coming from not just the stakeholders but the shareholders.[5] A November 2021 analysis of proxy proposals produced by the Conference Board and ESG analytics firm ESGAUGE, in collaboration with our firm and Rutgers University's Center for Corporate Law and Governance,[6] found that more proposals are being filed on these issues and going to a vote:

- Among companies on the Russell 3000 index, 348 proposals were filed on environmental and social issues in the first half of 2021, and 158 were voted on, up from 314 filed and 151 voted in the first half of 2020.
- Support for those proposals averaged 32% in 2021, up from 28% in 2020.
- The highest level of average support (69%) was recorded for proposals requiring companies to publicly disclose their workforce diversity data (EEO-1).[7]
- The second highest level of average support (61%) was recorded for proposals requiring companies to publicly disclose climate-related lobbying.

The belief that business must choose between doing good and doing well has finally been dispelled. Again, "it is no longer a nice-to-have; it's a must-have," Gaurdie Banister Jr., our chair at RRA, former CEO of Aera Energy, and a veteran member of many other boards, told me. "There was a time when it was more about eliminating risks so you could move forward in the business, but today it is a part of who you need to be, and you've got to be really clear about that." (Gaurdie is also a board member of chemicals giant Dow and natural gas distributor Enbridge, and a former member of the Tyson Foods and transportation solutions company Bristow Group.)

Top of the Agenda

It has been a long time coming. It has taken years for corporate governance practices to catch up with the reality on the ground. At RRA, we did a deep dive into the board's role in sustainable leadership, interviewing more than 130 corporate directors and C-suite directors around the world, surveying more than 1,500 additional corporate leaders, and conducting extensive analysis of executive and board-level talent recruitment and compensation practices. We learned that the will is there, but directors often struggle to decide how to act, and how ambitious to be.

Looking at the full and diverse landscape of board culture, Gaurdie is a little more circumspect. He likens some board directors to "frogs in water as it is being brought to the boil, not sensing how quickly they are getting cooked." But now they are feeling the heat and rethinking ways to become more proactive. Boards that were already leading on sustainability generally followed a road map built on issues of board leadership, composition, culture, purpose, strategy, risk alignment, structure, and process. Once a board decides it needs to act, directors often struggle to decide how to do so and how ambitious to be. As one board director told us, "Typical of a company at our level of maturation, we've done a lot on the sustainability front, but maybe not in the most sophisticated fashion."

Many boards expressed concern they were falling behind on this issue given the tsunami of SDG-related events. "Yesterday, sustainability was on the board agenda as a token to balance the social and environmental price of profit," said Steve Langton, who leads our Board and CEO Advisory Partners in the Asia Pacific region. "Today, it is a top board agenda because profit won't be possible again without it. The opinion of community, employees, customers, suppliers and, of course, shareholders now has collective power. Tomorrow, corporations won't have access to capital, talent, and brand trust without advanced and effective sustainability agendas and priorities."

Just as CEOs and the organizations they lead must be moonshotters, taking bold and decisive action, boards must do the same. Our research has shown that quickly going all-in on efforts such as investing in cleaner energy or pushing hard for reliable sustainability metrics, for example, may ultimately result in stronger long-term performance for companies. When assessing how corporations developed their diversity, equity, and inclusion efforts—a similar undertaking in many ways to sustainability—we learned that most companies take a linear and lengthy approach to building up their operations, adding elements slowly over 5 to 10 years. However, a small group of companies took a fast-track approach, investing heavily up-front to establish a mature set of operations and practices. These fast-track companies have quickly outpaced traditional ones, reaching maturity in about half the time.

The lesson for boards? Be courageous in your actions on matters as important as these and commit the organization to high levels of performance right from the start.

Seeking Alignment

There is a formula that can propel boards and management teams forward, faster, on matters of sustainability. One key element is alignment. There needs to be a shared understanding that sustainability is fundamentally about more than managing risk—it is integral to the people and profit centers of the business.

Gaurdie's great skill for getting there is asking the right, probing questions and never settling for the standard platitudes about going green or diversity that an individual thinks he wants to hear.

"It's about asking the CEO, 'What's your vision and your end game? Where do you want this company to be?' Then you test the extent to which the CEO, as well as other board directors, have conviction about it, or it's probably not going to happen. Quite frankly, it's just going to be another initiative."

A collaborative relationship between management and the board is essential for long-term success. Management identifies and prioritizes risks and opportunities in order to manage and disclose those issues as appropriate. At the same time, the board educates directors on the same risks and opportunities, integrates them into the board process, oversees the work of the company, and ratifies associated data, strategy, and goals. When this partnership works well, ESG initiatives are thoughtful and productive, which means they can become fully integrated into the business over the long term. When board and management struggle to reach alignment, however, ESG efforts risk becoming disjointed or unsuccessful.

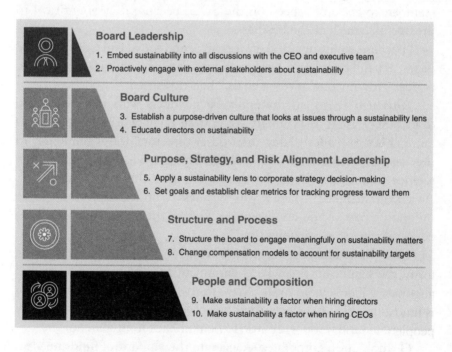

Board Leadership
1. Embed sustainability into all discussions with the CEO and executive team
2. Proactively engage with external stakeholders about sustainability

Board Culture
3. Establish a purpose-driven culture that looks at issues through a sustainability lens
4. Educate directors on sustainability

Purpose, Strategy, and Risk Alignment Leadership
5. Apply a sustainability lens to corporate strategy decision-making
6. Set goals and establish clear metrics for tracking progress toward them

Structure and Process
7. Structure the board to engage meaningfully on sustainability matters
8. Change compensation models to account for sustainability targets

People and Composition
9. Make sustainability a factor when hiring directors
10. Make sustainability a factor when hiring CEOs

Leif Johansson, chairman of the board of AstraZeneca, former board member at drugmaker Bristol-Myers Squibb, and former chairman of the European Round Table of Industrialists, had a few thoughts on this process when we talked about the swift and decisive way he and his "equally green-minded" AstraZeneca CEO Pascal Soriot made multibillion-dollar commitments on vaccine access and carbon emission reduction.

"Boards should do three things: we should do strategy, we should do governance, and we should do talent management to make sure that we have the right people to execute our strategy. I would certainly put the ESG issues in the strategy headline."

Leif put the emphasis on long-term strategic thinking. Again, boards must get away from thinking about sustainability goals in terms of compliance and view it as "an asset, something from which you can actually derive value."

But getting it done requires a certain board composition. Appointing single-purpose directors fragments the board and makes it difficult to build unity on sustainability. It is incumbent on *all* board members to get up to speed on the SDGs because they are critical to the overall health of the business.

"Because environmental, governance and social issues are strategic issues, as a full board member I would never accept that it's not my role to deal with any one of these goals," Leif explained.

Although there will naturally be members with more expertise than others, such as an audit committee chair who perhaps knows more about Sarbanes Oxley than other directors, for example, or, in the case of AstraZeneca, a well-known geneticist who chairs the science committee, "Don't let the experts steal the show," urged Leif. As a board member, "Make it your business to understand what's going on and be part of the conversation. Get in there, get interested, get educated, and start participating!"

Once they establish this cohesion within boards, decision-making about the significant financial commitment to sustainable projects and solutions will flow more easily. As we learned in Chapter 5, AstraZeneca invested and risked hundreds of millions of dollars advancing sustainability goals around the world with little to no pushback from shareholders.

"I think often corporates exaggerate the amount of funds needed. And they see spending $100 million as a fearful amount of money—an absolute barrier," Leif told me. "But it's all in how you look at it."

A likeminded board well-versed on sustainability can see the wider context. It takes less convincing to get its members to look past the absolute number and do a different kind of math, factoring in the cost of *not* spending that money or calculating the investment as an incremental increase in the cost of doing business somewhere along the supply chain. In the case of Maersk, for example, the increased cost of running containerships on clean fuel can be seen in terms of the extra pennies consumers would be willing to spend on that Nike shoe being shipped. For a drugmaker, "When you explain it's a 0.1% increase in spending on R&D as a percentage of sales, that great, big number doesn't seem so impossible to achieve," Leif explained.

Better Board Balance

US boards have come a long way in terms of gender diversity, according to a November 2021 report by Pay Governance,[8] an independent executive compensation advisory firm. Although there is still some distance to go, 30% of directors at S&P 500 companies are now women, up from 18% just five years ago. During the same period, female board members increased by a net amount of approximately 2,700, and, by contrast, male board members have declined by a net amount of approximately 1,900, a trend that is predicted to continue. These strides toward a balance of gender on boards are happening alongside nascent growing success of the recruitment of underrepresented minorities. Overall, it's positive trend in gender diversity that will serve to propel boards further along toward sustainable development goals.

Socially Conscious Cash

Again, boards are getting it. They realize that sustainability is not just a reputational imperative but a path to profitability. In fact, sustainability now attracts significant amounts of capital from lenders and large institutional investors.

Capital that would have been a struggle to access in 2020, for example, started to flow with surprising ease following November 2021's COP26 in Glasgow, where major organizations from around the globe pledged billions of dollars to fight climate change. As Hywel

Ball, United Kingdom Chair of EY told me, "It was amazing how much interest the banks showed when we moved our finance discussions from a normal facility to an 'ESG' one." By December of that year, EY announced it had secured an ESG-linked revolving credit facility (RCF) that was the first of its kind among the Big Four accounting firms in the UK, which includes KPMG, Deloitte, and PwC. The facility is based on the firm's commitment to carbon reduction, diversity, and society, and its performance against these targets will be measured annually to determine the interest rate, which could go up if they fail to deliver on their SDGs.

"It's not necessarily the price of the facility, but the availability of the credit, that's being driven by the flow of cash toward net-zero goals."

A whole investor ecosystem based on sustainability has evolved, from smaller research-based asset managers such as Netherlands-based Robeco, which is a world leader in sustainability investing, to the investor giant BlackRock, which has developed a suite of SDG-themed exchange-traded funds. As of 2020, roughly one-third of assets under management were based on ESG investment.[9] The popularity of this kind of marketplace, particularly among socially conscious,[10] younger investors, has even spawned a few impact-focused investment firms, such as Engine No. 1, which was founded in December 2020, made headlines when it campaigned to replace three ExxonMobil board directors, and launched its first ETF in June 2021.

Founded in 1939, asset manager Neuberger Berman is far from being a newcomer to sustainable investing, having developed its values-driven approach decades ahead of its competitors. Yet this early adopter has recently gone all-in; approximately 86% of the firm's assets under management were ESG integrated by 2021, compared with 60% in 2020, and just 25% in 2016.[11] (ESG integration, as defined by UN-backed coalition Principles for Responsible Investment, is "the explicit and systematic inclusion of ESG issues in investment analysis and investment decisions."[12])

With more than $447 billion assets under management as of March 2022 and a team of more than 2,500 professionals in 37 cities globally, Neuberger Berman is a relatively modest but mighty player in institutional investment and an early proponent of sustainable investments. Its size enables Neuberger Berman's team of asset managers to be nimble and accountable. And yet the thorough and data-driven system of analysis the firm developed is precisely why, in September 2021, China chose the firm to be the third US-owned asset manager to be allowed to operate within its borders.

"We were third behind a little firm called BlackRock," Neuberger Berman's CEO George Walker quipped when we spoke shortly after the announcement. Fidelity was the second firm chosen. China was specific about wanting only major global players, but it was hard for them to ignore Neuberger's performance record because "they wanted to strengthen their markets and their practices, particularly on sustainability."

Neuberger Berman asset managers aren't afraid to hold feet to the fire, looking past the greenwashing rhetoric and demanding real evidence of progress on sustainability issues. In fact, all analysts must include a note about sustainability in asset reports, and it must be packed with relevant detail. No exceptions. As George put it: "For example, don't just tell us that your employees are your number one asset; show us. Show us your retention rates; show us your workforce composition. It's okay if you aren't exactly where you want to be but show us where you are going and how you plan to get there. If you have a longer-term objective, break it down into near- and medium-term targets. Tell us what the mile markers are that we should be monitoring. We want to know that you are making real progress."

And for those who cannot show the right level of seriousness, Neuberger Berman wields the power of the intention letter in advance of a shareholder vote. Since 2020, the investment manager has been engaged in an advance proxy voting disclosure initiative, publicly explaining its voting rationale on key issues. Called "NB Votes," the initiative aims to address what is on the forefront of investors' minds, including diversity, human capital management, capital allocation, pay equity, racial equality, political contributions, and climate change. It included 31 meetings in the initiative in 2020 and increased that number to 62 meetings in 2021. These disclosures are in addition to the more than 4,600 engagement meetings with corporate management teams the firm conducted in 2021. But George was quick to push back on the idea that this was a form of investor activism.

"Reflecting back, company management teams valued the clarity of the explanation of our voting rationale as it enabled more robust dialogue with our investment professionals."

Hearing the investment management's heavily research-driven judgments on SDG issues enabled meaningful change. Or, as George put it to me, "When an investor is willing to speak up on an issue and explain its viewpoint well in advance of a shareholder vote with not only its vote intention but with a rationale note that says, 'We are opposing for x, y, and z reasons,' Clarke, it really starts to get attention."

Measure to Manage

There is a saying that what gets measured gets managed, so business metrics are critical for showing, rather than telling, progress in meeting their SDGs. Understanding the direct impact this proof of promises kept will have on cash flows, sustainable leaders have been striving for ways to ensure they have transparency and accountability—internally and based on standards set externally.

Internally, 3M holds its individual business units accountable for innovating on better products for the consumer and the environment by introducing sustainability KPIs into its new product development and launch process. Beginning in 2019, 100% of the company's new products (approximately 1,000 per year) are required to have a sustainability value commitment that demonstrates how the product drives impact for the greater good. The company measures the impact of this commitment and publicly reports on it annually to ensure transparency.

Finnish renewable energy company Neste Corp. has also embedded sustainability in its KPIs. So, for example, with CO_2 emissions cut by 2025 as one of its goals, projects that address cutting these emissions will have more value.

"We didn't only look at the return on investment but also *how* this brought us closer to our targets," Peter Vanacker, Neste's former CEO and president, explained.

PepsiCo incorporates environmental sustainability criteria into its capital expenditure filter, which is applied to all requests over $5 million. It reviews each request against business financial metrics and its ability to advance the business strategy, as well as for its impact (positive or negative) on environmental performance and its contribution to efforts to achieve the company's climate goal.

And Natura, the Brazilian beauty product manufacturer introduced in Chapter 2, holds everyone accountable; from its truck drivers to the C-suite executives, everyone is expected to help meet the SDGs. The transportation department is given a certain carbon budget, for example, and if it can't meet it by taking a certain route on a highway, they need to come up with an alternative delivery method. Natura's sales and marketing team are also tasked with ensuring that its 8 million sales representatives worldwide, mostly women from underserved communities, have access to education.

Executive compensation is tied to meeting certain measurable SDG goals. "If we don't meet those, it hurts our pockets," João Paulo Ferreira, Natura's CEO, told me, sharing how, in 2011, the financial targets were met but the sustainability goals were not, so no one got a bonus that year. "That's how you embed a sustainability goal; that's how they know it's important." Each year, Natura's metrics for success get more sophisticated and demanding. The leadership is continually challenging itself. That was the first and last time they missed their sustainability targets.

Natura's sustainability goals are so intertwined with business targets that it has issued its first P&L statement integrating commerce activities with the SDGs. It's a sophisticated level of accounting that shows in concrete terms the importance of sustainability to the business.

Setting the Standard

But the greater challenge has been standardizing the metrics of performance on sustainability issues for companies and industries all over the world. The result may not only be misleading but also can have unintended consequences when targets are not truly met or decisions are made based on an inaccurate picture. The resulting confusion can also be demoralizing for those on the frontlines who have been devoting their energies to more sustainable processes, projects, and products.

Several startups have attempted to answer this need, including pulsESG™, which has been developing an auditing system that can be integrated with customers' existing platforms (and which you will learn more about in Chapter 10). But a standard framework of measurement is also happening on global scale. During the World Economic Forum's Sustainable Development Impact Summit in 2021, a coalition of more than 50 multinationals announced the cocreation of a comprehensive metrics called stakeholder capitalism metrics, which created a set of data points that could be compared between companies of any region or industry.

The metrics that were developed include nonfinancial disclosures centered on people, planet, prosperity, and principles of governance, with measurements in pay equality, greenhouse gas emissions, board diversity, and other SDGs. They were also designed to be user-friendly and can be used within companies' existing ESG frameworks. So far, more than 100 companies have adopted this standardized approach, including Accenture, Bank of America, IBM, Unilever, Salesforce, PayPal, MasterCard, and many other Fortune 500 businesses.

The stakes for accurate and standardized metrics are high. Nothing can undermine even the most sincere efforts toward reaching sustainable goals more than a lack of credibility among internal stakeholders and investors. Incomplete or unreliable data, a lack of agreement on methodology, and what to measure and why have led to numerous allegations by advocacy groups, investors, and consumers of greenwashing, mislabeling, and miss-selling. Inadequate SDG risk measurements, which somehow overlooked major geopolitical red flags for years prior, were also blamed when certain corporations found themselves on the backfoot over the Russia-Ukraine conflict.

"As a leader you have got to make sure that those measures are reflective of the business strategy you are trying to follow," Hywel told me. "It has to flow and make sense."

Metrics are integral to this sustainable leader's three-point strategy to accelerate change:

- Allocation of capital
- Transparency and disclosure
- A way to be measured against our deliverables and held accountable

The problem is that even companies in the same industry with similar business models and market conditions in their global operations struggle to agree on metrics.

"If you look at the way the Big Four measure carbon at this moment, each seems completely different for ostensibly the same business," Hywel observed.

Arbitrary metrics or "a box-ticking exercise" don't do enough to move the needle forward or drive behavior that will help EY meet its public targets. Hywel has been collaborating with the Big Four and other corporations, both through the Embankment Project for Inclusive Capitalism and with the World Economic Forum, to establish clearer and more consistent standards. With so much money on the line and no time to waste, these frameworks are essential to hold business to account. He believes the announcement of the setup of the International Sustainability Standard Board (ISSB) at COP26 will be a huge step forward in establishing a globally consistent management framework.

"Whatever the metrics, suddenly this gets very real, very quick."

Sustainable Leadership Takeaways

1. It is a different world. Doing the right thing is now inextricably linked with corporate governance. It is sitting at the top of the board's agenda and not just one of many strategic goals.

2. Stop hesitating. Recent history proves that major decisions are powered through when the stakes are clear, and foot dragging risks damage to the brand that can do far more long-term damage to profits than the near-term financial exposure.

3. Aggressive actions yield better results. Be courageous in your decision-making as a board. Commit the organization to high levels of performance right from the start.

(*continued*)

4. Tie performance review, compensation, and bonuses to deliverance on appropriate and realistic SDG goals through specific metrics.

5. Strive for alignment. There needs to be a shared understanding that sustainability is integral to the people and profit centers of the business. A collaborative relationship between management and the board is essential for long-term success.

6. Grill the decision-makers, asking the right, probing questions, and never settling for the standard platitudes about going green or diversity that an individual thinks he wants to hear.

7. Make sustainability the responsibility of all board members. Appointing single-purpose directors fragments the board and makes it difficult to build unity. Because environmental, governance, and social issues are strategic, board members should participate fully in these discussions.

8. What gets measured gets managed, so business metrics are critical for showing, rather than telling, progress in meeting their SDGs, which will attract more investment.

9. Pay attention to evolving systems of measurement in your industry. Arbitrary metrics or "a box-ticking exercise" don't do enough to move the needle forward or drive behavior.

PART

IV

A Sustainable Future

10

Sustainable Startups

If you want something you've never had, you must be willing to do something you've never done.

—*Thomas Jefferson*

EACH SITTING ALONE at the top of a mountain, on an uninhabited island off the north coast of Sweden, members of H2 Green Steel's leadership team are encouraged to look out to sea, contemplate nature, and take stock of their lives. As part of the exercise—the company's version of a corporate off-site—they face north, east, south, and west by turns, taking in the view from all points of the compass. They then look inward to examine different aspects of their professional and personal selves as the Baltic wind howls furiously around them.

The 20 executives were recent recruits to a startup that aims to produce the world's first fossil-free steel, revolutionizing an industry. They arrived at the small island by boat, took an hour to walk around its circumference, then dispersed to find a spot where they could see no other human being or signs of development. They set up tents and then hunted for firewood, edible roots, berries, and whatever other items of survival they could rustle up from the nearby brush. And that was entirely the point, Henrik Henriksson, CEO of this highly disruptive startup whom you met in Chapter 5, explained months after his company made international headlines with its announcement that it would begin production of the first fossil-fuel-free steel by 2024.

"I know it sounds like mumbo-jumbo, but in Sweden we have a strong connection to Nature. It's kind of our religion," he told me.

It's all part of an onboarding process as Henrik brings more engineers, scientists, management, IT, and marketing talent into the fold of his rapidly growing and boldly innovative business. Although anyone attracted to such an intrinsically green business is likely going to have a sustainable mindset, Henrik wants his people to go deeper, experiencing the wilds of the Arctic circle on these thrice-yearly sojourns, so they never forget their purpose. Whether it is camping on a coastal island, boating on an inland lake, hiking up a glaciated mountain or through a vast boreal forest, they must spend three days communing with the landscape, each other, and their inner selves— cell phone free.

"It's not Navy SEAL training exactly," Henrik demurred. "But these simple exercises help them bring down the walls around them, so that they stand naked and vulnerable in the environment, though of course not literally! It helps them imprint images of Nature in their minds, so they can make that link to our values and all that we do."

As someone who has led both a startup-from-scratch industrial innovator and a legacy company (Swedish commercial vehicle manufacturer, Scania), Henrik knows all too well what it will take to bring people with him on his mission as his company grows at a rapid pace. So far, he has used his blank slate to recruit a fully diverse team, with individuals from 14 different countries; half his workforce, at the production and management levels, are women.

"We practice what we preach, and we would be stupid not to, because you can't attract 100% of the talent if you are not fully representative. We are building a steel mill of 2020, not 1970, so it's no longer a question of [being] able to lift 200 kilos."

Henrik has found the right people with the right competencies with relative ease thus far. Yet, he takes nothing for granted.

"One of my biggest lessons learned over the course of my career is that if you're going to build a culture, even though you are running around like crazy trying to sort out operational issues, you need to invest enough time on clarity of purpose, and then work throughout all levels of the organization to develop a corporate DNA that will stay with you as you grow."

■ ■ ■

In the previous chapters, I have dissected the qualities of the sustainable leader. I've shared examples of major multinationals that have made huge strides in transitioning to more sustainable business practices, through innovation, investment, the deliberate embedding of values through the culture of the corporation, the supply chain, and beyond. I've explored the whole mindset in multiple scenarios. But sustainable leaders who go on to found companies where sustainability is at the core—the entire mission of their products or services—are on another level. Sustainability is intrinsic to these businesses and their people. It is why they get up in the morning, although of course the aim is also to make a profit. Similar to all sustainable leaders with successful track records, sustainable *startup* leaders are as pragmatic as they are passionate because they must be. This is not a "transition," evolution, or large corporate experiment to feel good. These pioneers understand the need to show the world that sustainability is an economic opportunity *and* the right thing to do. It is as much about creating a business as it is about creating a movement.

It takes that much more passion, conviction, persistence, and entrepreneurship to launch a business that's born and steeped in sustainability goals because until now they have been that much harder to fund and grow. The leaders of sustainable startups must find a need or solve a problem that is solely focused on a sustainable goal or goals, then create a business model to make that sustainability sustainable.

These startups offer products and services that answer today's urgent needs, but their ability to generate profits and attract investment may be years out as they develop the technologies, build the markets, and educate the consumers. They offer solutions to problems as basic as doing laundry or washing and styling hair sustainably. Or they are answering complex, industry-wide needs, such as providing consistent and accurate metrics for tracking sustainability goals. Often, these startup leaders have taken a pay cut or left steady positions in traditional corporations because they felt they could do more in the whitespace, free of the constraints of a legacy business. They learned what works in their previous roles, and what doesn't, and combine that knowledge with a willingness to experiment, even if takes multiple failures to find success.

Rinse, Refill

Those are the roots of sustainable hair care company, Hairstory, which was conceived in 2015 by a group of industry veterans. These founders grew increasingly concerned not just by the packaging waste in products such as shampoo and conditioner, but the water-polluting sulphates in most hair care products, which tend to over-cleanse hair, stripping it of its natural oils. They started out trying to change the way consumers traditionally thought about shampoo, but quickly evolved into a pure sustainability play, creating a subscription platform, the Refill Club, that delivers its products in large refill pouches. The goal is to enable customers to consume nearly 90% less plastic and produce at least 80% less CO_2 emissions during cleansing compared with traditional shampoo products using its New Wash. Hairstory is transparent, avoiding vague greenwashing terms that are common in the industry, using only the safest and best ingredients in its product and packaging to "leave no trace."

"We hang our hat on the fact that it is fully biodegradable, Eli Halliwell, Hairstory's cofounder, CEO, and former senior executive at Estee Lauder, told me. "So when it goes down the drain, it's going to disappear."

When we spoke, Eli proudly waved a new fully recyclable, aluminum-free plastic pouch—the result of extensive research, investment, and prototyping to get the brand's carbon footprint down to almost zero.

"There is no such thing as perfection, and it you strive for perfection you will fail. It is always about continuous, iterative improvement. It's a journey, not a destination."

Eco Laundry Warrior

Brazilian business founder Humberto de Andrade Soares's sustainable laundry company, a Lavadeira, was born out of a similar rethink. Washing clothes, similar to washing hair, is another activity in our daily and weekly lives that can be extremely polluting and wastes copious amounts of water. Humberto comes from a culture where sheets and clothes are pressed daily.

"Brazilians like things well done and, until recently, even middle-class families could afford a maid to do this chore, with the washing machine constantly running," he explained.

But the country's economy shifted, and domestic workers were in short supply. The timing was perfect for an environmentally friendly and more efficient way to outsource this task. Humberto launched his business in 2013, after observing the success of online, direct-to-consumer services such as Dollar Shave. He studied his own market of São Paulo and realized that, with the right cloud-based software and Internet of Things (IoT) tools, he could create a home pickup and delivery service that tracked every item. To ensure there was a market for his idea, Humberto consulted with local families, learning their washing and dry cleaning habits, budget, and preferences, then offered a subscription-based, twice-weekly pickup and delivery service.

At its core a technology company, a Lavadeira isn't your average wash and fold. Each item is photographed and scanned using bar codes so each of the 10,000 or so items processed daily doesn't get lost and receives the appropriate treatment.

"Doing laundry is easy; garment logistics are not."

But the result of all this technological problem-solving is more than an Uber for laundry, because it enables customers to save up to 92% of their at-home water use, with a single washing machine doing the laundry of 500 households.

The startup, which received venture capital from Brazilian economist Group of Thirty member and former central banker Arminio Fraga, uses plant-based, biodegradable soaps with orange peel as their core ingredient. And predictive analytics track customers' fashion and wearing habits, along with the wear-and-tear on each item, to help each item last longer and limit textile waste.

Although the business took a hit during the pandemic, when Brazilian household budgets were forced to tighten, it is recovering, and Humberto hopes to franchise a Lavadeira throughout the country. Meanwhile, the serial entrepreneur, who is developing other sustainable business solutions, sees a distinction between a traditional business's sustainability approach and that of a sustainable startup.

"The difference is that [most legacy companies on a sustainability path] seek to promote positive environmental externalities and do less and less harm, but its products are often processed or use synthetic molecules. They are doing good, but I want to do more. I want to create products and services that are intrinsically sustainable."

Fueled by Philosophy

To that end, Humberto took some time during the pandemic lockdowns to study the great philosophers through the ages, from ancient Greek and Mesopotamian texts to the authors of the Age of Enlightenment to contemporary thinkers.

"I'm interested in the imperative of natural laws as they relate to human progress to understand how we can more fully live our interplay with Nature. To me, the idea of a sustainable business grows out of that principle, played out in the market."

Humberto's earnest studiousness is nothing unusual among this breed of business leader. During the course of my many interviews for this book, I discovered that sustainable CEOs tended to have a deeply philosophical bent. They are prolific readers who take the time to educate themselves first. Henrik describes a 2012 meeting with Johan Rockstrom, a Swedish professor and joint director of research for the Potsdam Institute for Climate Impact Research in Germany as an "almost religious experience." The professor became a mentor of sorts to Henrik, who soaked up his science-based conclusions about how, for example, resilience can be built back into water-scarce lands.

"The way Professor Rockstrom explained the dangerous sort of path that we were on, but at the same time he said it is possible to change the trajectory, transformed my way of thinking. He told me we can do this, but we need to work together. And we need to work fast. Even then he was clear about how important the corporate side of the global transformation was for us to become sustainable as a society."

That sense of urgency works as a kind of fuel, particularly for leaders of sustainable startups who could use the extra kindling to burn through all the other challenges they typically face. It takes a degree of evangelism to galvanize their stakeholders and maintain that purpose-driven mindset in the face of repeated rejections and setbacks. Many start small, growing organically and scaling through the sophisticated use of technology platforms, AI, and the IoT, often of their own innovation. The impact they ultimately have on their industries is profound, but it can often be a struggle to ramp up the business.

Closet Refresh

James Reinhardt, CEO and founder of the circular fashion company thredUP, began his business while still in college as a peer-to-peer platform for consumers to exchange their gently used quality fashion items. At the time, Reinhardt wasn't necessarily thinking in terms of sustainability in the sense of reducing the water waste and carbon footprint of one of the world's most polluting industries. He just wanted a way to clear out and refresh his closet so that his J. Crew shirts and Banana Republic pants wouldn't contribute to the problem of fashion waste. But the overwhelmingly positive response from sustainably minded young fashion customers, who were only too eager to find a more sophisticated alternative to shopping in thrift stores, inspired him to pivot the business and create a giant consumer platform, or what he terms a "managed marketplace" for circular fashion.

The problem was, most of the investment community had not yet seen the value in what they saw as little more than an e-commerce version of a giant thrift shop and consignment store. One by one, his plans to raise capital to hire the experts to build the AI technology and physical infrastructure—a resale-as-service platform—that could track, manage, warehouse, and ship millions of unique clothing items met with flat nos.

"I was rejected 27 times by investors before receiving my first yes," he told the NASDAQ's newsletter after a successful IPO in March 2021.

"In those moments, I learned the hard way that you can't convince investors to change their minds. I had to find an investor who believed in my vision and felt passionate about thredUP's purpose. All you need is one yes, but with a pregnant wife at home and my savings poured into this company, it was hard to keep that in mind."

He eventually got that yes and raised $300 million, growing the startup into the largest online circular fashion business in the world because it helps existing retailers in their resale business in addition to millions of consumers looking to trade or buy the nearly new clothing, accessories, and shoes. At the time of writing, thredUP received about 100,000 items daily, putting a decent dent into textile waste, which makes up more than 6% of municipal waste in the US, according to the Environmental Protection Agency. The fashion industry is one of the world's worst polluters in terms of water use and waste. About 3 million tons of used clothing gets incinerated each year, and another 10 million tons goes to landfills—both processes release copious amounts of greenhouse gasses.[1]

The company's technological solutions to reducing fashion waste have led to a wave of other circular fashion companies, from luxury consignment platform The RealReal to Poshmark. They're even inspiring traditional fashion houses such as Gucci to go circular.

"Before thredUP, there had been no innovation in online thrift since eBay and Craigslist," Reinhardt told Nasdaq Entrepreneurial Center in an interview.[2] "We built the backbone of resale on the internet, applying technology and cutting-edge logistics to make it easy for anyone to sell their clothes and refresh their closet responsibly."

But as was the case with Green Steel, it could not have happened without the right people. Reinhardt considers one of the most important aspects of his role as a sustainable entrepreneurial leader to be his ability to attract, develop, and retain talent with the skillsets to help scale the vision. He hired the same engineers who developed Netflix's DVD warehouses to create thredUp's unique processing system—technological thinkers with the same mission mindset.

"As a leader, it's important to set the tone for the company and hire smart to maintain company culture as you grow," he said, echoing Henrik. "It's important to me to show up with a positive attitude every day, and I see that reflected in the team members around me."

So, it's not just his vision, it's their *shared* vision, that will lead the change in the way the world shops and thinks about ownership, at least when it comes to fashion.

"ThredUP's mission is to inspire a new generation to think secondhand first. My dream is a Clean Out bag in every closet, and thredUP as a household name across America—the first place people look when they want an amazing outfit for a great price. It's crazy to look back 10 years and see how far we've come, and I think as long as we keep an eye toward why we started this business in the first place, we will get there."

Against the Wind

But, again, it can take time, and multiple setbacks, to reach the destination. If you think traditional businesses face headwinds, consider what a sustainable, social enterprise is up against. According to an often-quoted study by the Failure Institute,[3] which followed a population of 115 for-profit social entrepreneurs in Mexico, only 17% of these businesses survived beyond three years. The business leaders who were surveyed faced obstacles such as the fact that they are operating in countries that are behind the regulatory curve when it comes to sustainability. They also struggled to find the necessary resources and infrastructure to grow their businesses.

Many of their teams did not have adequate fundraising skills, in addition to the challenge of attracting and convincing investors to put money into relatively small enterprises. Impact investors tend to be interested in more advanced businesses that can turn a profit in a shorter time frame. As a result, founders and CEOs of early-stage sustainable businesses lean on forms of capital that can become expensive over time, giving away equity, which makes it difficult for them to attract future investment.[4]

Another trap, particularly for founders of sustainable startups, can be giving away too much equity to investors and diluting the original vision. As Hairstory's Eli advised, "Generate cash as quickly as possible on your own so that you can be self-sustaining. . . . Never give away too much power to your investors because they may act out of fear and push you to do stupid things."

Thankfully, as I write this, the business environment and economic opportunities for sustainable startup leaders are changing fast, with less chance of scared money compromising founding values. Corporations and investors are actively looking to partner, acquire, or invest in sustainable startups that can help them leapfrog toward their own SDG goals. According to a January 2022 survey,[5] 25% of US CEOs with acquisition plans said their primary goal was to strengthen performance on their SDG goals.

"That's the first time I've seen ESG and sustainability show up as a significant driver of deals," observed *Fortune* magazine columnist Alan Murray,[6] noting that the desire to improve their sustainability footprint outstripped digitization, operational improvements, and talent acquisition.

Consider Silicon Valley company pulsESG™, a public benefit corporation founded in 2021 to help enterprises measure, disclose, and improve their ESG footprint through its proprietary software-as-service platform. The startup, which was barely in development when we spoke in October 2021, had little difficulty raising $9.5 million in seed capital. Although sustainability metric companies exist in an increasingly crowded field, pulsESG™ provides auditable and accurate analytics that can be integrated with their customers' existing platforms. The startup up has built software architecture that can be adapted to the changing regulatory environment while providing more in-depth analysis, empowering companies to make more informed ESG decisions.

Its cofounders, tech veterans Murat Sönmez and Inderjeet Singh, are highly regarded in the tech investment community. Murat was a member of the founding team at TIBCO Software and led it past the billion-dollar revenue mark as head of its customer-facing operations. He later joined the managing board of the World Economic Forum in Switzerland, leading its global business community engagement efforts, and subsequently established and helmed its global technology policy network out of San Francisco. Inderjeet, the startup's software savant, was most recently responsible for Oracle's middleware and cloud platform. He was head of engineering at TIBCO, where he led all product functions. Inderjeet was also part of the founding team for Velosel, a Silicon Valley venture–funded startup, acquired by TIBCO.

The pair are trusted by impact investors because of their long track records of success in their industries.

"Murat and Inderjeet stand apart with the completeness of their vision, passion for impact, and unparalleled combined experience in successfully scaling startups," said Rick Kushel, cofounder and general partner of FINTOP Capital.

But why would these two leaders, who could write their own tickets to work anywhere within Big Tech, want to take a huge pay cut for the risks and comparatively small gains of a startup?

"When Murat first approached me, I was intrigued by the complexity of the problem, and the potential to genuinely impact the world. But the more I researched this thing, the more I realized it was not just an opportunity to create a transformative software as a service platform from scratch, but also to create a force for good," Inderjeet explained.

The clincher? "I checked with my teenage daughters, and for the first time, they both wanted to work for this company," he joked.

Small but Significant

The appetite for companies that can help other businesses address their social and environmental sustainability goals is growing exponentially, as evidenced by leading cloud service provider Blackbaud's $750 million acquisition of EVERFI, which uses technology to address social challenges through education programs in companies, schools, and communities. The merger, which took place in early 2022, turns the two businesses into a sustainability servicing powerhouse. Blackbaud already had more than 100 Fortune 500 customers on its YourCause platform— software that helps companies manage their giving and volunteering programs, which are increasingly being used to drive SDG goals and attract talent.

"It's getting [woven] into every business we see," Blackbaud CEO Mike Gianoni told *Fortune* magazine.[7] EVERFI has noticed a similar explosion of demand for what it terms

(*continued*)

"impact-as-a-service"—technology and software that enables companies to, as its founder and CEO Tom Davidson writes, "tackle and report on intractable social issues at scale."[8]

The technology is initially focusing on employee diversity, inclusion, unconscious bias, and harassment prevention training, as well as upskilling courses to ensure career advancement opportunities. It also offers data-driven solutions for tracking and reducing greenhouse gas emissions.

Although *Fortune* columnist Alan Murray doesn't generally devote much ink to deals of this relatively small size, in his CEO Daily platform, this is one business with huge potential, and others concur. EVERFI counts TPG's The Rise Fund, as well as tech powerhouses Jeff Bezos, Eric Schmidt, and Evan Williams, among its early investors.

Investor A-List

One could easily assume that a typical sustainable startup leader is young, full of idealism, and prone to making rookie mistakes—an environmental activist, perhaps, who cooked up a sustainable business idea in a college dorm room. But increasingly the opposite is true. Many are seasoned business leaders, such as Murat and Inderjeet, with a thorough understanding of the practical underpinnings necessary to achieve such lofty goals.

Henrik of H2 Green Steel arrived in the sustainable startup world with a long pedigree of leadership positions at major multinational companies. He served for 24 years at Scania, the last six as CEO. He was a member of the executive team at TRATON SE, a subsidiary of the Volkswagen Group, and serves on the board of directors at Electrolux; carmaker SAAB; Hexagon, a global IT company; and Creades, the Swedish investment company that focuses on small- to medium-sized businesses. He also serves on the board of the Confederation of Swedish Enterprise.

Henrik came onto my radar late in 2021 on a whistle-stop tour of Scandinavia, where I met with several sustainable leaders from Danish shipping giant Maersk: CEO Søren Skou; Svein Tore Holsether, CEO of the Norwegian fertilizer company Yara; and Mads Nipper, CEO of Danish multinational energy company Orsted. At the end of my interview with Søren at the Maersk headquarters in Copenhagen he mentioned the startup. I subsequently learned that Henrik had raised 86 million euros in its series A of financing from major multinational corporations including Maersk and its ownership, AP Møller; Scania; one of the Ikea foundations; Spotify; and several other multinational firms; as well as one of Europe's most powerful business families, the Wallenbergs.

"There's a level of expertise that is starting to emerge and create pathways for sustainability in tough industries like cement, steel, transportation, and this is what we need now," Søren told me, referring not just to Henrik's company but also to dozens of Scandinavian companies that are pressing ahead with solutions and experiments in hard-to-abate industries that could be transformational in terms of their production methods.

Those putting money into H2 Green Steel recognized the enormous potential value of a fossil fuel–free steel in a vast array of products, from skyscrapers to heavy machinery, ships, trains, buses, furniture, and cars. Mercedes-Benz was so enthusiastic, it became an equity partner with a single-digit million-dollar amount and became a preferred partner with plans to launch green steel in various vehicle models by 2025.

"It's the perfect mix of investors that we want to have," Henrik told the *Financial Times* in a May 2021 interview.[9] "There is a willingness to help this industry transform, and an understanding that this is urgent."

The startup's goals are unabashedly bold, aiming to do no less than decarbonize the European steel industry—one of the largest emitters of carbon dioxide in the world. H2GS started from scratch in 2020 a large-scale production in Boden-Luleå, Norrbotten, a remote site just south of the Arctic Circle. As I write this, the company has 50 diverse employees from all over the world who joined the company because they share the same mission mindset as Henrik, and he predicted their ranks would swell to about 2,000 by 2023, in lockstep with his plans for phase B financing to raise another $2.84 billion.[10]

Henrik attributes his success in raising capital to the story he told about his "customers' customers." He already had examples of the sustainability needs throughout the supply chains at Scania, Electrolux, and Volkswagen.

"There was a market there, and the fact that I had good insight coming from one of those big industries that would buy our steel certainly helped," he told me.

The pitch had to be good because green steel will be about 25% more expensive.

"The first question is always, 'Will they pay for it?'" said Henrik.

But he knew potential buyers such as Scania had already done the math. Under his leadership, they had already weighed the price of more expensive components versus the cost of doing less toward their sustainability goals.

"The next question is, how will you finance this?"

Henrik followed the model of Northvolt, another sustainable Swedish startup founded in 2016, which produces recyclable, lithium ion batteries and technology for electric vehicles. The company's financial engineering involved a balance of enlightened and deep-pocketed investors with lucrative, long-term customer contracts, with investors and customers overlapping in some cases. As of mid-2021, Northvolt had raised $6.5 billion in debt and equity, and it secured more than $27 billion worth of contracts.

"And the final thing is competence. You need to show investors a trustworthy plan of how you recruit from all over the world."

That is where Henrik's slightly unconventional approach to building a sense of purpose—sticking chief technology officers from Italy and mining experts from India on top of a breezy bluff in the Baltic—comes in.

Green New Industrial Revolution

Of course, as an ambitious *industrial* startup, it will take more funding and more bodies—blue collar, technical, and management expertise—than a typical fledgling business to achieve its goals. H2 Green Steel aims to ramp up to an annual 5 million tons of emissions-free steel by the end of the decade by using electric arc furnaces powered by green hydrogen, which is produced with renewable energy, instead of the traditional method of burning coke.

It's one of a few sustainable startups, as well as legacy steel producers, that are jumping into the race. H2 Green Steel is part of a movement. To be sure, its projected output is minuscule compared with the whole of the $2.5 trillion global steel industry, which at the time of writing was projected to grow to 1.9 billion metric tons.[11] But its impact through proof of concept goes way beyond the numbers. The steel industry, which accounts for 7% to 9% of the world's direct fossil fuel emissions, greater than India's total output, is facing increasing scrutiny. The International Energy Agency is calling for the steel industry to slash emissions in half by the middle of this century to meet global climate goals. But for sustainable leaders such as Henrik, that is not good enough. Solutions need to happen now and cannot wait until the EU's 2050 deadline.

H2 Green Steel is at the forefront of this industrial revolution 2.0. Another close contender is Hybrit, also Swedish, which plans to produce 2.7 million tons of fossil-free sponge iron to be used by its part owner, and Scandinavian steel manufacturing giant SSAB, as well as other steel producers. (It is also partnering with Vattenfall, the Swedish power multinational, and Swedish state-owned mining company LKAB.) Although Hybrit will not go into full production until 2026, it started a pilot plant in the northern coastal town of Lulea and had already made its first delivery of the green steel to truck maker Volvo AB, which planned to use the fossil-free steel in a line of trucks and machinery before the end of 2021.

But Henrik welcomes the competition.

"We don't see ourselves as disrupters so much as enablers, to show the incumbent industry what is possible. Now come on, join us!"

Sustainable Leadership Takeaways

1. Build a corporate DNA, a strong culture that will stay with you as you grow. Be intentional about it. Those who join you may well already share your sustainability

(continued)

mindset, but deepen and refine it so that your team never loses that sense of mission despite the complexities that come with scaling operations and facing obstacles.

2. Use your clean slate to start out your organization as fully diverse. Don't limit yourself by drawing from one culture or set of experiences. You will be better able to attract the best talent from around the world when they can already see or hear themselves represented in your organization.

3. Balance passion with pragmatism. Sustainable startup leaders understand the need to show the world that sustainability is as much an economic opportunity as it is the right thing to do.

4. Expect setbacks but persist nevertheless, because the deep-pocketed investors are finally catching on. It's traditionally been harder to finance sustainable startups because they are by their very nature small and have tended to grow organically rather than through acquisition. But when you develop a sound financial plan and a product or service that is intrinsically sustainable and fulfills an urgent need, the resources will come.

5. Leverage cutting-edge technologies and proprietary solutions to create the intrinsically sustainable service or product that is the basis of your business. Build something that can have applications across industries and product categories and contribute to a sustainable movement.

6. Pay attention to what others have done in your sector successfully, as Henrik did when he borrowed freely from Northvolt's financial model.

7. Use your whitespace not just to create something new out of whole cloth but to learn from the wins and losses of more established businesses.

11

A Generation of Nudgers

People seem to think this is an issue that can be solved another time, but there is no other time.

—*Zoe, 14, student, during a UK school strike for the climate, February 2019*[1]

IN 2010, WHEN she was in the middle of her master's degree, Blanca Brambila Perez got the call that her father had been kidnapped. It was a common occurrence in Mexico, where many kidnapping victims don't survive. After 10 days of tense negotiations, her family paid the ransom and Blanca's father was returned safely home. But the incident shook her.

"From that moment on, I started to see a bigger picture," recalled Blanca. "I had this passion to make the world a safer place."

Blanca, similar to many people her age, had been drawn to sustainable businesses long before this life-changing event. Throughout college and soon after graduating with a marketing degree she held various positions promoting "environmentally friendly" companies, including a small, new "green" label brand at a cement company. But the kidnapping ignited something powerful in Blanca, who became acutely aware of the fragility of our existence. She wanted to have a more direct impact on her community, so she switched from the private sector and took a job with an NGO that focused on providing legal and psychological advice to crime victims, as well as citizen engagement.

Then, in 2015, she was invited to apply for a sustainability department manager role at Heineken Mexico. They were looking for someone to manage the sustainability agenda for the company. Blanca saw it as her chance to have a broader impact and "change the world one company at a time."

Bright, eloquent, and bursting with energy, Blanca quickly rose through the organization, becoming director of sustainability for all of Heineken Mexico's operations, including the new Chihuahua plant, the brewer's largest and most sustainable production facility in the world. The more issues surrounding sustainability she took on, whether societal or environmental, the stronger her voice became. As a sustainability and resource manager, she presided over multiple successful initiatives within Heineken's operations, including "Every Drop Counts," which raised awareness about the water-stressed states where their breweries are located, and proved that it was possible to raise production while reducing water consumption. Mexico is now considered the number-one operating center for Heineken worldwide in terms of volume and water efficiency, using only 2.6 liters of water per liter of beer produced.

In part due to Blanca's advocacy, Heineken Mexico became the model for water care globally, participating in international forums that share good practices and knowledge with all the other Heineken breweries. Beyond saving water, Heineken Mexico contributed to local ecosystems, balancing and restoring the habitats to their original state, and reducing their water footprint as much as possible, ultimately offsetting more than 2.4 million cubic meters of water in the Monterrey, Toluca, Guadalajara, and Tecate plants while improving the quality of residual water returned to the environment.

"They called me the water lady," Blanca recalled with pride.

The success of these green initiatives caught the attention of Heineken's CEO Dolf van den Brink, whom you met in Chapter 3. As head of operations in Mexico before he was promoted to the C-suite, he was acutely aware of the many associates on the ground who helped him pivot the company to a more sustainable future. Soon after he became CEO, in the usual corporate shake-up that happens when there's a change in leadership at the top, he assigned Blanca to the role of global head of circularity at the Amsterdam headquarters. It would be part of her job description to inspire and nudge global and OpCo teams to step it up.

"They were sitting on the fence," Dolf told me. "No one was fiercely opposed to it, but surely no one was pushing."

That was another theme that emerged from my conversation with sustainable leaders: the fence sitters tend to be the bigger obstacles to transition than the naysayers. At least with the naysayers, you know where you stand.

When I spoke with Blanca toward the end of 2021, she was just finishing her fourth month in her new position and coming through the other side of countless exhaustive conversations about whether the strategy developed in Mexico, where Heineken has 16,000 employees, could work at the global and local levels of the organization.

"Mexico's strategy is serving as the guiding principle for Heineken globally that I am helping to define, and that is something that fills me with a lot of pride," said Blanca, who is now affectionately known as "the circularity lady."

■ ■ ■

Blanca is one among hundreds of thousands of future sustainable leaders who are driving the demand for change from the bottom up and taking action to accelerate sustainability goals in significant ways. She is what we call a next-generation leader—those who today are sitting one or two levels below the C-suite but with all the potential to one day make it on to the executive team or to the corner office, if the stars align.

These next-generation leaders are leading the charge on sustainability action because, for them, it's personal. A key finding from our sustainability study covering 9,000 respondents in 11 countries was that, in the past two years, 40% of next-generation leaders had personally taken on three or more initiatives to improve environmental outcomes for their organizations. They have a track record and an understanding of what works in real-world, practical terms within the nexus of profitability and sustainability. I cannot think of a more hopeful indicator for our future, because when it is their turn to lead, they will have had extensive experience delivering sustainability results.

By the time next-generation sustainable leaders have ascended to the C-suite, they'll have overcome barriers, created followership, worked with the right partner organizations, and embedded sustainability into business strategies, which is exactly what is required. In effect, these individuals will know a lot more about how to reach and exceed sustainability goals than most at the top of corporations today. They will grab that baton and run farther, faster, for a much greater impact. As a result, we will be able to accelerate and scale the transition exponentially.

I cannot emphasize enough how important it is that we, as leaders, listen and learn from the younger generation. Recognize these sparks that create the fires of enthusiasm. Talking to these bright young stars—the people who light the most fires—can drive change far more than anything you, as a senior leader, can say at a town hall, a board meeting, or in a podium speech. I guarantee that you have far more sparks among these more junior ranks than in your C-suite. Look for them, encourage them, and build that fire for sustainability from the ground up.

This demographic, for whom doing right cannot be decoupled from overall business targets, were mostly born this way—as passionate activists. Collectively and individually, these next-generation leaders have become a powerful force for change. At a minimum, they are inspiring their CEOs and other more senior executives to do better, if only to attract likeminded young talent who increasingly shun organizations that are falling behind on their sustainability goals. Still others are coming up with fresh new ideas and executing in ways that are yielding tangible results across multiple business functions. Even more exciting is that, sitting behind these next-generation leaders, is a whole new generation who are even more sustainably minded—people who were born into an awareness of the perils our planet faces. They have been taught about environmental and social issues in school and are openly frustrated by the apparent complacency of their parents' generation. For them, sustainability is not about what looks good. It is not just about mitigating risk or creating long-term value for stakeholders. It is visceral.

No Plastic Bags!

In 2010, a full decade before New York State introduced its Bag Waste Reduction Law, banning all plastic carry-out bags in stores, my youngest child and son, Liam, was already on it. He and my wife, Whitney, had seen the documentary about plastic waste called *Bag It* and they were appalled. Liam and his older siblings went out to buy groceries at our local supermarket and forgot to bring along reusable bags. It was a big shop, because they were stocking up for the weekend and there was a lot to carry home, but Liam was adamant about refusing to accept the plastic bags the store was willing to provide for free.

"Aw, come on, Liam!" my daughter Devon, who was 12, pleaded with her younger brother. "How can we possibly bring all this stuff back without bags?"

"Not with plastic, *nuh-uuuh!*" Liam shouted. "Don't you know where they end up? Landfills, the rivers, the oceans . . . and it will be all our fault!"

Liam had won his point, because his siblings agreed with him and because they wanted to avoid any further public scene in a store which we as a family regularly frequented. Each of my four children, including my twin girls, Caitlin and Morgan, stuffed bags and pockets to bursting with fresh produce, soap, paper towels, cereal boxes, and so on. Then they made the four-Manhattan-block trek back to our apartment, stopping several times along the way to pick up the escaped jug of milk and bag of cookies from the pavement. (Luckily, no eggs were broken in the process.)

Around the Dinner Table

Most of the leaders I spoke with in researching this book have had similar experiences with their own children. Sustainability, more specifically environmental SDGs, has been the stuff of heated conversations at dinner with their children, to the point in my own home of fists pounding and occasionally knocking over some cutlery! In fact, it's how many CEOs come to their own sustainable mindset, as we discussed in Chapter 3. They must face the harsh scrutiny of their offspring. And, as they help their middle schooler with a homework assignment on diversity or the environment, they start asking themselves the tough questions.

Julie Sweet, Chair and CEO of Accenture, a professional services company that has led the way globally of sustainability goals, and whom you met in Chapter 6, told me environmental SDGs were not her passion until her children started learning about climate change in school.

"They were born into it, so it was those conversations at mealtimes that sparked my own passion and commitment to climate goals," Julie shared. "They really worked on me!"

For Leif Johansson, chairman of pharmaceutical giant AstraZeneca, it was at the breakfast table back in the 1990s, when he was CEO of white goods manufacturer Electrolux. He had just learned about the CFC emissions of its refrigerators when his daughter, who was 14 at the time, asked him to explain the company's position. He fumbled for an acceptable answer until she rolled her eyes and said: "How about using your intelligence to argue what can and should be done rather than try to defend the wrong thing?" (Not surprisingly, she grew up to be a lawyer.)

It was an early awakening for Leif, who has been doing a gut-check with the younger generation ever since.

"I'm often telling people that if you don't know whether you are doing the right thing, try explaining it at the breakfast table to your family. And if you don't pass that test, don't continue what you are doing. Change your path."

Shining Sea

My own transformation happened to take place at sea, where many of my profound experiences in life have occurred. On the previous pages I described my near-death encounter with a shipping container. Yes, that moment jolted me awake, but perhaps what opened my eyes even more fully to the perils of climate change was an experience I had sailing across the Atlantic with my mostly grown children three years later, in 2018.

We'd already been at sea for several days when we came across what was to me the familiar glow of phosphorescence while sailing at night. My kids oohed and awed over this stunning natural phenomenon. But I felt somewhat deflated when it occurred to me that I used to see those diamonds sparkle through the inky blue less than 200 miles off the coast versus a thousand miles. The oceans had suffered so much damage from pollution since I first sailed across that it took days before the waters lit up beneath our vessel with glowing plankton. My son and three daughters didn't get to have the same experience I had. And if nothing is done about the contamination of the oceans, those natural points of light might disappear altogether.

Fired Up

These moments growing up, combined with what she had learned in the classroom and her own kind-hearted, idealistic nature, are what shaped my daughter Devon's views on sustainability and turned her into something of a conference room warrior, in the best possible way. It wasn't long after she joined Visa's marketing department in San Francisco as a junior associate that she made her voice heard. Devon had been tasked with researching the benefits of being a purpose-driven company. Although Visa has always embedded sound corporate values, Devon and her team found being purpose-driven perhaps was not always clearly articulated either internally or externally.

"Visa at its core has always been intrinsically purpose-driven through the impact we have on people's lives every day, yet we have always been viewed as a credit card company," Devon shared with me.

The more she researched the importance of being purpose-driven, diving into the numbers and discovering how much better purpose-driven businesses performed over the long-term, the more inspired she was to create impact. She soon realized that perhaps Visa's leadership team weren't connecting the dots between their sustainability and purpose-driven actions, which were happening, and their broader messaging. Visa could be so much more impactful, particularly with a younger audience, with a universal understanding of who they were and what they were all about. It wasn't that anyone was actively against having a purpose, but in this day and age being purpose-driven has become a modern corporate imperative, so as my daughter continued to present her research findings, her sense of urgency came through.

"Having a clear purpose is not just a trend. It leads to higher financial performance, better workforce retention, higher levels of innovation and creativity. I, along with my peers, want to be inspired by a sense of purpose—through the brands we interact with and the companies we work for!"

Devon started creating case studies that were sent the department heads to create a broader understanding of the importance of being purpose-driven, ultimately making a case for corporate purpose. Leaders at Visa listened and gave her an unprecedented opportunity by enabling Devon to make her voice heard. Soon she was asked to make a live presentation at a department town hall. Next, she was called on to make several more videos and appearances to educate her colleagues across multiple functions in the 20,500-employee multinational. A year and a half later, Devon has moved up the ranks, from associate to analyst to department manager. Early on in her career she has been identified as a potential sustainable leader of the future, and I am full of admiration for her conviction and focus. Fatherly pride? Absolutely!

But I am also impressed with the way Visa's leadership saw my daughter's zeal as an opportunity. That's the way to do it as an organization. Ask questions. Make the effort to really listen to what your youngest stakeholders have to say by uplifting and advocating for future leaders. Hear them, develop them with skills training and exposure to other areas of the business, reward them with more responsibilities and larger roles. Give them the tools they need to turn that passion into productive action, then ask yourself again, "Are you listening?"

Research shows that millennials are 5.3 times[2] more likely to stay on in a company when they feel connected to their employer's purpose, but it must be more than some top-down mission statement. It's a living, breathing thing—a dialogue that engages them and seeks out their perspective. As leader, as CEO, you will win this transition to sustainability when you treat your youngest talent as the invaluable resource they are.

Our youngest associates are at the vanguard as the most engaged drivers of sustainability action. They are in the trenches, overcoming barriers and often yielding impressive results. Organizations looking to accelerate their sustainability agenda should proactively find ways to empower, recognize, and incentivize their future executives.

One example of a leader who mined this gold by actively listening is Peter Vanacker, former CEO and president of Finland-based renewable fuel producer Neste Corp. Each quarter, his employees were encouraged to participate in a "Way Forward" survey—a series of 10 questions that aimed to gauge their sentiment about various aspects of the operating culture, including whether the company was spending enough time on its purpose. Roughly 80% to 90% of Neste's more than 5,000 employees completed the questionnaire, giving Peter and his leadership team deeper insights into the priorities and concerns of Neste's most important stakeholder group, including its youngest associates and future leaders. The fact that this was an ongoing metric also kept their awareness current, which, as we explored in Chapter 6, was paramount to the process of embedding sustainability. Neste's leaders were never operating on a set of assumptions about sentiment that had changed or gone stale. Neste also regularly held open workshops where everyone was free to participate, further deepening awareness about the company's sustainability goals

"We took time to articulate a culture to fit our new purpose, so when we launched the survey, engagement was very high, especially among our younger employees," Peter, who is now CEO of LyondellBasell, told me.

The Engine Room

Future executives, such as Blanca, are well-positioned to carry the sustainability mantle, overcome barriers, change culture, and devise better products and services for their customers and consumers. Whether motivated by personal passions and core values, or delegated responsibilities from their managers, these up-and-comers are driving sustainability initiatives into the fabric of the organization.

But it takes conscious effort and eyes open to cultivate and activate that talent. Charles O. "Chad" Holliday Jr., former chairman of Bank of America, former CEO of DuPont, current board member at John Deere, and coauthor of *Walking the Talk*,[3] which makes the business case for sustainability, shared with me how, as CEO, he made a point of going to a business school to present a strategy for his company, then invited pushback from the students, finding real gems of ideas within their dissenting opinions.

"I learned a lot, and, by the way, the students in China and South Korea gave me some of the best pushback in the world!"

Chad, who spoke with me on a next-generation leadership panel in Glasgow at the 2021 UN Climate Change Conference, offered another great piece of advice for retaining and developing younger talent: understand that it's not just about financial compensation. Recognize their pride and balance the tangible rewards with the intangible.

Chad was reminded of this the day before our conversation, when he was counseling a young executive in a hard-to-abate industry about a prospective change in roles. The new job would have been a lateral move, but with exciting opportunities for advancement and more pay. Yet the candidate didn't want to make the switch. He felt he was making an impact where he was, and it was all that mattered to him.

"I'd rather stay in this job no matter what else I could do because I want to see this through," he told Chad. "It's important to me."

From what Chad has observed, more young people feel this way. So, in order to attract and retain them, it's even more important to change how performance is recognized. All those bonus calculations and KPIs of the past need to shift toward something more holistic than financial results and inclusive of sustainability goals.

"It all comes down to the definition of performance," Chad told me.

Bottom Up

At Heineken, Dolf, who is young for a chief executive at a multinational company though not exactly a millennial, seems to be finding that balance and creating a culture for future sustainable leaders. Blanca is just one example of many eager next-generation leaders at Heineken Mexico who have been recognized, encouraged, and promoted. Internally, Dolf and his leadership team called Blanca, and executives like her, the "generation of nudgers."

Another nudger is Hector Garcia Montemayor, a young associate in the procurement department of Heineken's Monterrey brewery. Hector had been obsessing about ways to operate more sustainably ever since he was in college studying to become an engineer. He became deeply concerned when, on a visit to his family's farm in the

Monterrey countryside, he noticed how polluted the river and surrounding landscape had become from exhaust fumes, litter, and contaminants. By then a major highway had been constructed next to the property, and the bucolic paradise was ruined. Even the family's livestock—free-range goats and chickens—had begun dying off.

"That gave me a reality check," Hector told me.

Ever since then he'd been looking for ways to use his engineering and innovation skills to improve the world around him.

"Unfortunately, I couldn't stop using my car, but there was something I could do that would have a broader impact."

It just so happened that Heineken Mexico's plants were based in some of the most water-stressed areas of the county. How it used water affected not just the water sources themselves but also the entire surrounding communities. Heineken had already begun to reduce water waste within the brewing process, so Hector analyzed the entire supply chain to figure out other areas of water consumption and landed on textiles, which happens to be among the top three wasters and polluters of water among all industries, particularly cotton.

Hector made the calculation and realized that Heineken Mexico went through 200,000 pieces of clothing for its uniforms each year, with just one pair of jeans consuming 5,000 liters of water. The bulk of these uniforms wore out after several months and were discarded. Using his engineering brain, Hector applied the concept of a circular economy to this granular piece of operations, logistically thinking through which types of garments, fabrics, and trimmings could be reprocessed (about 40%), then finding a reliable external partner willing and able to pull off circular uniform production at scale. He found a company in Vietnam with the capacity to recycle uniforms of Heineken Mexico's truckdrivers.

Beyond Barley to Bar

Of course, Hector's innovation went beyond Heineken Mexico's transportation division. Once he achieved proof of concept, other departments, even other beverage companies, started focusing on these less direct elements of the supply chain to reduce waste, pollution, and carbon emissions. And Heineken's partner, the Vietnamese garment producer, could spread this idea of circular uniform production to its other customers. In other words, it went viral.

Meanwhile, Hector's creative solution caught the attention of his bosses. He was invited to compete in an annual sustainability contest, which was open to any employee in local operations under 30. Each nudger was given five minutes to pitch an idea for renewables and circularity. The best five concepts were selected for the attention of senior management, who then chose a winner to fly to the Netherlands to participate in the Nudge Global Impact Challenge. In that aspirational, United Nations–like setting, organized by an NGO, these Mexican associates could meet and discuss their ideas with 100 other participants from other organizations around the world.

"Can you imagine, you're 28 years old and you've never been outside of Mexico, and suddenly you find yourself surrounded by all these other bright young minds, who are as idealistic and determined as you are, how inspiring, energizing and empowering that must feel?"

Dolf believed that the contest would be a good way to identify the next generation of sustainable leaders while also gaining insights on potential sustainability practices and innovations from executive and management-track employees with direct experience at all levels of the supply chain. In a way, he was nudging himself. At first, his colleagues in senior management, who were neutral on the subject, chuckled at the thought of some ill-conceived, feel-good experiments that would likely never be implemented. But year after year, "we were inundated," Dolf told me. And not only were many of the ideas good, they were practicable, having been carefully mapped out in ways that could easily be implemented throughout Heineken Mexico's supply chain.

Hector's idea won. Similar to Blanca and several of his colleagues, Hector has since been promoted from the field office in Mexico to Amsterdam's global headquarters, where he is now the global data buyer for business services. He continues to search for more indirect ways to do business sustainably.

"We tend to only look at the barley-to-bar concept, but even in my category there are ways to have a positive impact on the environment," observed Hector, who is researching methods for reducing energy use at the brewer's international data and service centers.

Each in their own way, Blanca and Hector were triggers for major operational changes. On their respective journeys as sustainable leaders at the lower and middle management levels, they started by asking themselves what they, as individuals, could do to change. Then they thought through how they could drive change beyond their roles based on their individual strengths and skillsets. Blanca, the advocate, enlisted a core group of believers to go out into the farthest reaches of the beer giant to evangelize on the twin topics of sustainability and circularity. Hector, meanwhile, demonstrated what could be done at the procurement level. Through intrapreneurship, openly and actively encouraged by Heineken's leadership, he's showing and bringing others along with him, leveraging their eagerness and ideas, triggering change in practices across the company, the industry, the government, and NGOs.

"It starts with tips and tricks," Hector told me. "Then you enhance your concept, bring it to the next level, which triggers more people to get involved and think about their own sustainable solutions."

Hector shows; Blanca tells. We need both, and we need more young leaders like them, who can lead faster, differently, and with greater impact. In many respects, they are more impatient for results. But that's what makes this group such an invaluable resource as we push that much harder toward meeting our sustainability goals. Sustainability success is now inextricably linked to the challenge of attracting young talent into the organization and consumers to the brand.

Competition for talent, particularly young, sustainability-oriented workers, is fierce as companies around the world and across industries scramble to meet net-zero emissions goals.[4] Meanwhile, the "great resignation" that followed the global pandemic proves beyond a doubt that employees of all generations need to find meaning in what they do every day beyond financial compensation. According to a survey by global realtor JLL,[5] 70% of millennials prefer to work for companies with strong sustainability agendas—a strong indication that Gen Zers want the same. So, although we have been focused on actions throughout much of this book, do not overlook myriad ways a well-deserved reputation for attaining your SDGs will attract the brightest and the best. Their peers will talk. They will be drawn to your organization through strong internal and external messaging or something visible at the operations level, such as a culturally diverse workforce or a physical workspace that recycles and uses renewable energy, for example.

But, as I mentioned in Chapter 6, it's not enough just to have this demographic working within your organization. All that passion and skill has nowhere to go without empowerment. You need to give them the tools long before they've ascended to the upper reaches of management. You must foster, focus, and reward them with visibility. And your side of the conversation with these associates needs to be authentic and backed up with concrete actions.

Soul Searching

As in all things related to sustainable leadership, whether attracting, developing, or retaining talent, the answers are not obvious. They are complex. It takes courage and a willingness to listen to potential successors all the way down the line, even when they challenge you. Be open and curious enough to seek out their opinions.

You also need to be flexible, thinking in terms of scenarios rather than following a one-point plan, which is why it is even more important to accept challenges from the new angles being offered by your youngest associates. Give those who are involved in sustainability the assurance that this is a viable way to the top that isn't necessarily measured in the bottom line. Make sure you are being seen to invest in sustainable solutions to problems, because, trust me, as a father to Gen Zers, they have a nose for the inauthentic. No empty gestures.

As Laurence Debroux, board member of Danish pharmaceutical multinational Novo Nordisk and former CFO of Heineken, put it when she spoke at our Glasgow panel: "Find clarity of purpose not just as a communication exercise but as part of a deep soul search of what the company and its people are here for."

To that end, have the humility to look outside your four walls for answers, ask for help, and work collectively to build that message. Your young and high-potential associates will respect you more when you check your ego and bring more candor to the conversation.

"Have the ability to say, 'I don't know everything, and I need some help,'" said Laurence.

Finally, demand results and accountability. Encourage experimentation, but make sure the ideas are solid, researched, and embedded in the strategy. If sustainability issues are top of the list of agenda topics, act accordingly and make sure that priority is seen, felt, and heard throughout the organization.

Above all, don't wait passively for this pipeline of talent to ascend through the ranks. Those of us who already sit in the C-suite must reinvent ourselves now, at both the executive and boardroom levels.

"The next generation of sustainable leadership is up at the door, knocking, and saying we are not going fast enough," Laurence observed.

So, it is up to all of us, though I am grateful that there are Blancas, Devons, and Hectors in our midst to pick up the pace.

"If I may be poetic, I am trying to be the spark that starts the flame, the fire that catches," Hector told me.

How many sparks do you see in your organization? Are you giving them enough oxygen to ignite? The more these embers can turn into flames, the brighter our future will be.

Sustainable Leadership Takeaways

1. Incentivize your next-generation leaders to come up with sustainable solutions, then create forums where those ideas can be taken seriously and heard.

2. Even in the junior ranks, young associates can be powerful forces for positive change, collectively and individually.

3. The younger they are, the more proactive and activist employees tend to be on environmental issues. For them, it is visceral. Find ways to harness this passion.

4. Give next-generation leaders the tools they need to turn that passion into productive action. Hear them, develop them with skills training and exposure to other areas of the business, then reward them with more responsibilities and larger roles.

(continued)

5. Be authentic. Millennials are five times more likely to stay on in a company when they feel connected to their employer's purpose, but it must be more than some top-down mission statement.

6. Clearly define the metrics and value creation of sustainable solutions so your young leaders don't feel like they are tilting at windmills. Reward them for taking on the tough issues that may not yield results in the near term.

7. Stay current with how your younger associates are thinking and feeling. Leverage tools such as employee surveys and town halls. Rather than operate on a set of assumptions about sentiment, make sure you understand where you stand.

8. Understand that it is not just about financial compensation. Recognize their pride and balance the tangible rewards with the intangible. As leader, you will win this transition to sustainability when you treat your youngest talent as the invaluable resource they are.

Epilogue

Legacy and Learnings for a Sustainable Future

What you leave behind is not what is engraved in stone monuments, but what is woven into the lives of others.

—*Pericles*

IT HAS BEEN energizing and eye-opening to share these stories. The opportunity to learn from dozens of leaders globally who are implementing bold actions for people and planet has also been humbling. Motivational speaker, the late William Arthur Ward, put it this way: "The pessimist complains about the wind; the optimist expects it to change; the leader adjusts the sails." Looking back on this process, my only regret is not having the space to capture every insight and observation from these in-depth conversations. Through their candor, the pioneering individuals I met with gave me an embarrassment of riches. But the overall takeaway from more than two years of research is this: my hunch about the potential impact of sustainable leadership when first brainstorming with then-UNGC leader Lise Kingo at Davos in 2019 (before the world changed forever) was right. Not only has our

189

hypothesis borne out, our hopes and expectations for how we can move the needle forward have been far exceeded by what is actually happening across industries and geographies. There is now no doubt in my mind that we *can* deliver people and profits with the planet. The energy is not just what they are doing, but how they are multiplying future sustainable leaders through success, trial, error, and communication.

There are clear pathways, fire tested with experience and guide-posted with careful metrics, with numerous pioneers demonstrating the possible in real time. Yes, we *can* make an impact, and we must! It has been proven exponentially through the stories of these change-makers I have shared with you in this book that sustainability is not just sustainable, it is good business, and the only way forward for the long-term health of your organization.

Of course I realize that these chapters do not read like a conventional leadership book. The proclamations and commitments for 2030, 2040, and 2050 seemed so far out to me that I wanted to understand what leaders were doing *now*. Could we learn from them and spread the word to accelerate sustainable leadership impact? So I started calling the leaders I admired most; I asked for their stories and whom they admired most. What I received from them, when put down on paper, almost read like a novel, though entirely nonfiction. And I admit I have been anything but dry in my approach to this topic, which is deeply personal to me. The anecdotes I have given you run the gamut of emotion, even a little comedy, because these are human issues that touch us all, no matter where we sit as stakeholders. But these are not mere words designed to keep you turning the pages. Each narrative has been intentionally underpinned with entirely pragmatic business strategies and solutions. Make no mistake, this is your practical guide to getting it done.

It all comes down to being able to translate a vision into solid and lasting business outcomes. Because increasing crop yields in sub-Saharan Africa with lower-emission fertilizer or achieving full circulatory at a brewing plant in Monterrey, Mexico, economically empowering women in India through guar cultivation, or investing billions in ships that run on clean fuels are illustrations that it is possible to achieve all three Ps—people, planet, and profits—when you truly commit. Think about it. Many of these actions began 5, even 10, years ago, well before there was complete buy-in from boards and investors. Imagine how much more can happen with the will that exists today?

It takes a leader who can integrate social and environmental considerations into business strategy, making the long-term sustainability and the resilience of our world a top business priority, while also delivering financial success. Colin Mayer, author and professor at the Saïd Business School at the University of Oxford, defined the purpose of business this way: "producing profitable solutions from the problems of people and planet, and not profiting from creating problems."[1]

A business cannot be driven solely by profits. Profits must be a derivative of solutions that serve the greater good. Sustainable leaders get the fact that sustainability and resilience and profits are not in separate buckets. One cannot exist without the other.

The stories you have just read serve to exemplify sustainable leadership in action. They also illustrate that the greatest thing we can do is identify, develop, and accelerate sustainable leaders. The existing scores of sustainable CEOs taking action at the Fortune 500 level is not enough. Your individual success is not enough. In order to accelerate change at the faster pace that's required, we need identify, teach, and developing multiples of leaders. We must make sure that the multiplicity exists for many generations to come.

That requires humbling yourself to learn from those who may not share your level of seniority. As Henry Timms, president of New York's famed Lincoln Center, notes in his book, *New Power*,[2] the power of today is no longer hierarchical. It is "open, participatory, and peer driven," channeling through many levels of an organization and essentially democratizing influence and decision-making. We are all at the same level on the subject of sustainability, which has become a unifying opportunity for leaders to listen, learn, and be decisive, even in a highly ambiguous world. It is a flattening topic, pushing from the bottom and listening from the top. So it is incumbent on those of us who are in more senior positions to commit to listen, engage, create opportunities, and take risks on those high-potential associates who are younger, at earlier stages of their careers, and further down in the organization. Young talent like Blanca Brambila Perez, that accomplished executive at Heineken whom you met in Chapter 11.

As a leadership advisor and former CEO, I want to be known as someone who created an environment that enables these high-potential individuals. I want my legacy to translate into opportunity for them by providing the funding, the approvals, the initiative, and the faster decision-making necessary for them to succeed. I have an obligation with the balance sheet, the budget, and the board approval to make it work. In my chief executive role, I was empowered to tap the CFO and our Chief Marketing Officer to create these kinds of frameworks, openings, and opportunities so that the Blancas of the world can bring their energy, idealism, and time to act on the sustainability goals. That is my obligation. And the responsibility of the younger and next-generation leaders—the aspiring CEOs—is to speak up, jump in. Acquire the practical skills and seek out mentors. Contribute to the outcomes and provide feedback. Push from the bottom. Because the Blancas and Clarkes must learn together, working shoulder to shoulder, on these most pressing issues of our lifetime.

Whether you are a CEO or a board director thinking about your legacy, the same overarching lessons, or ultimate takeaways, apply:

- **Know that this starts with you.** Sustainability action cannot happen without sustainable leaders. You now face a once-in-a-generation opportunity to step up and help solve the pressing challenges in our societies and economies. That may feel like an unattainable goal. But as we've seen in the pages of this book, it can be done. Our future depends on the decisions you make today. It all starts with you.
- **Commit to a wholesale embrace of sustainability.** The time of talking the talk is over; we have to walk the walk. Moving mission statements are not enough. Integrating sustainability across your strategy and operations, while anchoring it to your company's purpose, must become standard procedure. Avoid sidelining sustainability to specific people or departments. It has to be a living, breathing thing that is seen, heard, and felt across every function and operational level.
- **Don't be afraid to be the new kid.** There is nobility in admitting what you do not know. Embark on the endless sustainability learning curve. Every conversation you have with an employee,

client, outside expert, or external stakeholder is an opportunity to gain invaluable new insights. Surround yourself with mentors and people who will challenge what you think you know.

- **Resist becoming a 100 percenter.** You will lose the race if you try to get everything perfect before you start. When you are too deep in the detail you risk losing passion for the big picture. Don't spend months or years trying to obtain information that is failsafe. Find enough good data through experiments and pilots to make a decision. Greater than the risk of failure is not moving fast enough toward your sustainability goals.

- **Take a fresh look at your leadership team.** Who is on your leadership team, and how that leadership team operates together, has the potential to enable or torpedo progress. Take a candid view of your top team's perceptions of sustainability. Identify issues that may contribute to an unwillingness or inability to make it a core strategic objective, such as deference to hierarchy, risk aversion, or being stuck in the past. Identify the fence sitters, because they can be far more dangerous than naysayers. Pull them off the fence and make them declare themselves.

- **Make sustainability everyone's job.** Start at the top of the house; ensure the board and senior management make sustainability mindset and experience a key criterion when selecting and promoting leaders. Beyond this, updating selection frameworks to measure every new hire's sustainable leadership track record is the fastest way to embed a culture of sustainability and shared sense of purpose.

- **Raise the bar for success.** Set high expectations that everyone from frontline workers to department heads and C-suite leaders must contribute to meeting your sustainability vision. Embed sustainability across everyone's KPIs and tie compensation and bonuses to realistic sustainability outcomes.

- **Become a collaborator-in-chief.** The sense of urgency for sustainability is now so universal that someone, somewhere, is also working on the problem you are trying to solve. Engage with those who have different skills and experiences from you, even if that means partnering with experts outside your business or industry. External organizations such as nonprofits or academic institutions can also bring a sense of credibility to your vision, smoothing the way by overcoming community distrust or resentment.

- **Listen and learn from younger generations.** Frontline employees have much to teach us. In fact, we are leading when we are seeking their input. Incentivize your people to come up with sustainable solutions, then create forums where those ideas can be taken seriously. Hear them, develop them, and give them the training and tools they need to turn that passion into productive action— then reward them with more responsibilities and larger roles.
- **Build your bench of future sustainable leaders.** The shift to sustainable business will not happen in one CEO tenure alone. Your legacy as a leader will depend on your ability to identify and develop the pipeline of future sustainable leaders in your ranks who can continue the journey you started. These people are within your organizational walls (virtual or otherwise). Go find them, go develop them, and go add them to your succession plans. It starts now.

And, if you're a next-generation leader aspiring to become a C-suite leader, there are steps you can take to accelerate your organization's sustainability journey—and your career.

- **Make your voice heard.** You have much to teach those at the helm of organizations today. Find opportunities to share your passion for sustainability—and your ideas for how your organization can become more sustainable. Employee engagement surveys, town halls, and sustainability competitions are a good place to start, but always make sure you combine your passion with practical skills to develop and implement real-world solutions.
- **Show the business case.** For you, sustainability and business go hand-in-hand. But not everyone has this innate appreciation. Help your leaders understand that sustainability transformation is not just the right thing to do, but the smart thing to do. Demonstrate your business case for action by showing how sustainable thinking can boost the bottom line through more innovation, better products, and greater efficiencies.
- **Raise your hand for global experiences.** There are multiple pathways to becoming a sustainable leader, all equally powerful.

Some are born, others have an epiphany, many evolve over time. As our research shows, many leaders with a track record of integrating sustainability into the business have international experience, which exposes them to multiple cultures and helps them develop a more well-rounded understanding of how business works.

- **Think beyond linear career paths.** Cross-functional experience can prime you to think more sustainably, offering you a broader perspective on your business and industry. Notably, many sustainable leaders we talked to had experience in supply chain and operations, where they could see the direct impact on the ground and among workers of their sustainable strategies.
- **Hone your sustainable leadership credentials:**
  o **Multilevel systems thinking.** Sustainable leaders understand how their organization fits within wider economic, social, and environmental systems. Take time to understand your organization's relationship to the wider world—and how it is uniquely placed to help move the dial on the greatest challenges it faces today.
  o **Stakeholder inclusion.** Sustainable leaders actively engage stakeholders—from employees and customers to governments and investors. Do not operate in a bubble. Actively seek to understand a wide range of viewpoints when making decisions. This will require high degrees of empathy, humility, and authenticity. If you don't have these skills yet, develop them fast!
  o **Disruptive innovation.** The best sustainable leaders are those who can cut through bureaucracy to drive breakthrough innovation—and stay the course in the face of setbacks. Don't rely on what you already know or what worked in the past. Proactively gather new information and challenge yourself to strike a different path. Question traditional approaches and ask why it cannot be done differently.
  o **Long-term activation.** Sustainable leaders think in decades, not years. Always think about the big picture. Set audacious goals. The path to meeting them will not be easy. You'll need a great deal of courage and resilience to stay the course in the face of setbacks—and you'll need to get comfortable making decisions that will be unpopular with short-term-orientated stakeholders.

- **Listen and learn.** Open yourself up to learning. Many of the sustainable leaders we met intentionally surrounded themselves with people who challenged what they thought they knew. In other words, they set themselves up to receive new ways of thinking. Seek to acquire experiences, training, mentors, and partners who can deepen your awareness.
- **Don't fear mistakes.** You are not omniscient. Nor should anyone expect you to be. We are all going to make mistakes as we navigate the complex issues of sustainability. What matters more is your ability to be learn from mistakes, quickly correct course, and apply those lessons to future decision-making. Commit to honing your learning quotient (LQ). It will be one of the single-biggest determiners of your success as a sustainable leader.

And if I can leave you with one final thought, it is this. I was on a panel recently with Thomas Buberl, the CEO of AXA, the French multinational insurance company with 149,000 employees. I had the opportunity to ask him a question that has been uppermost on my mind, because it was something that had come up again and again, in many countries and languages. The phrase *fence sitters* was universal.

"These are the people who are the hardest to deal with because they sit back quietly, And, if you fail, they say, 'I told you so.' And if you win, they say, 'Oh, I was in favor of this all along.' So do you have any advice for handling them?"

Thomas did not hesitate with his answer:

The fence sitter model is not very sustainable, because you can hide in the short term, but you cannot hide in the medium term. At the end of the day, when we talk about sustainability, it is not about the box you have checked or the nice slide show you have produced. It's about results. As an investor, an underwriter, I will want to know your plan. You're at x degrees now, you need to get to 1.5, so how exactly do you get there? Which initiative, which measurement, which time frame? So the fence sitter has to declare him- or herself quickly or be pulled down from the fence. So stop wasting time. Climb down and play the game.

Notes

Chapter 1

1. https://www.russellreynolds.com/en/insights/divides-and-dividends
2. https://www.unep.org/resources/emissions-gap-report-2019
3. https://www.iucn.org/resources/issues-briefs/marine-plastic-pollution
4. https://www.ft.com/content/27c2c8c4-89be-4744-ac6c-bf4bb9d349bc
5. https://www.edelman.com/news-awards/2020-edelman-trust-barometer
6. https://www.edelman.com/research/trust-2020-spring-update
7. https://www.edelman.com/trust/2021-trust-barometer#:~:text=While%20the%20world,ethical%20and%20competent
8. https://www.robeco.com/media/4/4/0/440e5de2086735e4922318667e442163_20211101-robeco-strengthens-swiss-distribution-team_tcm17-32269.pdf
9. https://www.nytimes.com/2018/01/15/business/dealbook/blackrock-laurence-fink-letter.html
10. Data from Duke Energy.

Chapter 2

1. https://www.naturaeco.com/press-release/natura-co-unveils-its-commitment-to-life-for-2030/

Chapter 3

1. https://hayatlife.com/2021/01/06/ilham-kadri-solvay-ceo-fortune/
2. https://www.solvay.com/en/article/solvay-cares-and-heres-how-it-shows
3. https://mss-p-053-delivery.sitecorecontenthub.cloud/api/public/content/ungc-rra-leadership-for-the-decade-of-action-2020?v=c5c4747b
4. https://mss-p-053-delivery.sitecorecontenthub.cloud/api/public/content/ungc-rra-leadership-for-the-decade-of-action-2020?v=c5c4747b
5. https://www.marieclaire.com/career-advice/a28428318/google-chief-sustainability-officer-kate-brandt-data-centers/

Chapter 4

1. https://www.infineon.com/cms/en/discoveries/electrified-ships/
2. https://www.infineon.com/cms/en/discoveries/electrified-ships/
3. https://www.iea.org/news/new-iea-study-examines-the-future-of-the-ammonia-industry-amid-efforts-to-reach-net-zero-emissions
4. Data from Svein.
5. Data from Svein.
6. https://www.wsj.com/news/collection/sustainably-managed-companies-2020-2efa9094
7. https://www.mahindra.com/news-room/mahindrariseat75/mahindras-triple-bottom-line-approach-to-sustainability
8. https://www.mahindra.com/me-magazine/rise-for-good.html
9. https://www.ft.com/content/28e22386-a11c-11e6-891e-abe238dee8e2

Chapter 5

1. https://www.epa.gov/greenvehicles/fast-facts-transportation-greenhouse-gas-emissions
2. https://www.theguardian.com/business/2021/mar/26/how-the-astrazeneca-vaccine-became-a-political-football-and-a-pr-disaster
3. https://www.adlittle.com/sites/default/files/prism/1996_q4_24-28.pdf
4. https://www.thelancet.com/journals/lanres/article/PIIS2213-2600(21)00511-7/fulltext#:~:text=We%20estimated%20that%20the%20global,cases%2C%20using%20the%20LLN%20definition
5. https://www.who.int/news-room/fact-sheets/detail/asthma

6. https://www.joorney.com/news/4-transformative-lessons-for-modern-businesses-from-accenture-ceo-julie-sweet/
7. https://time.com/6125315/bernard-looney-bp-ceo-interview/

Chapter 6

1. https://www.weforum.org/reports/global-gender-gap-report-2021/
2. https://archive.dhakatribune.com/magazine/weekend-tribune/2017/05/04/nibedita
3. https://asiapacific.unwomen.org/en/countries/Bangladesh.
4. https://www.russellreynolds.com/en/insights/divides-and-dividends/foreword-alan-jope/
5. https://www.russellreynolds.com/en/insights/divides-and-dividends/foreword-alan-jope
6. Personal conversation.
7. https://newsroom.accenture.com/news/accenture-reports-very-strong-first-quarter-results-and-raises-business-outlook-for-fiscal-2022.htm#:~:text=NEW%20YORK%3B%20Dec.,the%20same%20period%20last%20year

Chapter 7

1. https://www.bloomberg.com/features/2020-green-30/

Chapter 8

1. https://www.reuters.com/article/us-climate-change-shipping/maersk-aims-for-carbon-neutral-container-shipping-in-2023-idUSKBN2AH0ZA
2. https://www.maritime-executive.com/article/maersk-keppel-and-yara-join-forces-for-ammonia-bunkering-in-singapore

Chapter 9

1. https://www.nytimes.com/article/russia-invasion-companies.html
2. https://www.shell.com/media/news-and-media-releases/2022/shell-announces-intent-to-withdraw-from-russian-oil-and-gas.html
3. https://www.russellreynolds.com/en/insights/podcasts/episode-7-leadership-reimagined

4. https://www.russellreynolds.com/en/insights/articles/the-nomco-chairs-view-on-sustainability
5. https://fortune.com/2022/02/15/shareholders-proxy-proposals-esg-conference-board-esgauge-ceo-daily/
6. https://www.conference-board.org/press/proxy-season-2022
7. https://www.conference-board.org/research/shareholder-voting/2022-proxy-season-preview
8. https://www.paygovernance.com/viewpoints/women-on-boards-the-u-s-corporate-journey-towards-gender-diversity?tpcc=nlceodaily
9. https://www.marketwatch.com/story/esg-investing-now-accounts-for-one-third-of-total-u-s-assets-under-management-11605626611
10. https://www.ft.com/content/14012ae6-6a3d-43fe-82c9-4c5378dc974c
11. https://www.nb.com/en/global/esg/philosophy
12. https://www.unpri.org/fixed-income/what-is-esg-integration/3052.article#:~:text=The%20PRI%20defines%20ESG%20integration,social%2C%20and%20governance%20(ESG)

Chapter 10

1. https://www.greenamerica.org/unraveling-fashion-industry/what-really-happens-unwanted-clothes
2. https://thecenter.nasdaq.org/faces-of-entrepreneurship-james-reinhart-thredup/
3. https://thefailureinstitute.com/wp-content/uploads/2017/04/Causes-of-failure-in-social-enterprises-low-res.pdf
4. https://www.nesst.org/nesst/2019/why-do-social-enterprises-fail
5. https://www.ey.com/en_us/ceo/ceo-survey-2022-us-findings
6. https://fortune.com/2022/01/12/esg-sustainability-mergers-acquisitions-ceo-daily/
7. https://fortune.com/2022/01/04/blackbaud-everfi-esg-demand-ceo-daily/
8. https://fortune.com/2021/06/07/impact-as-a-service-iaas-social-environmental-impact-everfi-rise-fund/
9. https://www.ft.com/content/ee91775f-0310-4e1b-b162-ffdf6e066757
10. https://www.ft.com/content/ee91775f-0310-4e1b-b162-ffdf6e066757
11. https://www.statista.com/statistics/209343/steel-production-in-the-us/

Chapter 11

1. http://www.die-klimaschutz-baustelle.de/quotes_climate_change_youth.html
2. https://www.pwc.com/us/en/about-us/corporate-responsibility/assets/pwc-putting-purpose-to-work-purpose-survey-report.pdf
3. https://www.routledge.com/Walking-the-Talk-The-Business-Case-for-Sustainable-Development/r-Holliday-Schmidheiny-Watts/p/book/9781874719502
4. https://www.ft.com/content/63a1fed0-384b-4390-b53a-f54630904c0c
5. https://sigearth.com/gen-z-makes-sustainability-important-for-all-businesses/

Epilogue

1. https://www.thebritishacademy.ac.uk/programmes/future-of-the-corporation/#:~:text=Professor%20Colin%20Mayer%2C%20the%20Academic,not%20profiting%20from%20creating%20problems
2. https://www.amazon.com/New-Power-Persuade-Mobilize-Connected/dp/110197110X/ref=asc_df_110197110X/?tag=hyprod-20&linkCode=df0&hvadid=312045876164&hvpos=&hvnetw=g&hvrand=1082731016491515661&hvpone=&hvptwo=&hvqmt=&hvdev=c&hvdvcmdl=&hvlocint=&hvlocphy=9060351&hvtargid=pla-597043634108&psc=1

About the Author

CLARKE MURPHY IS a leadership expert with an unshakeable belief that business executives have the power to change our world for the better.

At Russell Reynolds Associates, a global leadership advisory firm, Clarke advises the world's top companies on leadership strategies that fuel profitable growth and value for all stakeholders. He has fascinating insights into how business leaders around the world are embracing the sustainability agenda and using their position to solve the greatest social and economic challenges of our time.

Clarke's passion for sustainability began with a near-death experience while crossing the Atlantic. When his boat almost hit a huge container that had dropped from a cargo ship, he realized how important it was for companies to think about planet and people, not just profits. This moment of truth propelled Clarke to seek every opportunity to change the rhetoric about what it means to be a successful leader today.

His work on sustainable leadership has been published by *Bloomberg*, the *Wall Street Journal*, and the World Economic Forum. Clarke is also an in-demand keynote speaker at headline sustainability conferences, including the United Nations Global Compact's Leaders

Summit and the World Economic Forum's Sustainable Development Impact Summit.

Since 2021, Clarke has cohosted the *Redefiners* podcast, interviewing courageous leaders who are redefining their organizations—and themselves—to deliver extraordinary results.

Index